NEAR INDIA'S HEART

an account of Free Church of Scotland Mission Work
in India during the 20th Century

Anne M. Urquhart

THE KNOX PRESS [EDINBURGH]

THE KNOX PRESS [EDINBURGH]
15 North Bank Street, Edinburgh EH1 2LS

First Published 1990

ISBN 0 904422 25 9

PRINTED AND BOUND IN GREAT BRITAIN
BY McCORQUODALE (SCOTLAND) LTD.

NEAR
INDIA'S
HEART

NOTE

Accuracy of sketches and maps in this volume is approximate only. The boundaries of some countries are under dispute.

Contents

Introduction

At midnight, a villager called us to see his wife who was ill at home.

Setting out from the hospital, I knew which road to take out of Lakhnadon but not where to turn off for their village. From behind me in the jeep came directions, "Towards the sunrise, at the mango tree."

There was no moonlight, far less a hint of sunrise! And what would distinguish a **mango** tree from all the others along the road? Amazed at my ignorance, the guide took us there safely.

Twenty years later, when offered the work of recording the history of the Free Church of Scotland's witness at the centre of India in the twentieth century, I thought I knew the landmarks well. But even to tell the story has not proved easy, far less to understand and respond to the challenges. We thank the Lord for being our guide so far. We want to listen more closely to his continuing direction, given in various ways. May the story help us to learn, and to honour him for his love and faithfulness.

This book attempts to give more than **facts**. Something of the **feel** of life in India is provided by the interludes between the main chapters.

Although the Foreign Missions' Board of the Free Church of Scotland commissioned the book in 1985, and now sends it out, the interpretation of events, where attempted, is inevitably my own.

Three young artists – Janet Fraser, Naomi Miller and Norman Shaw – have lightened the text with their line drawings. Ian MacIver prepared the maps of India. Several of the camera studies – some vintage – by a variety of missionaries and their visitors have been reproduced by George Thomson. If it were not for the help of Gavin and Janet Smith, during daffodil time 1989 in beautiful Arran, I might still be immersed in mounds of manuscript. My sincere thanks to these people and to all who have encouraged me along the way.

thirst

Ram Das appears as a character in the pamphlet "Cool Water in Drought", written in 1965 at the request of the Foreign Missions' Board. It describes the impact of Christian witness at the heart of India then. Although conditions are different now as the century draws to a close, the same challenge, to communicate the gospel effectively, continues today.

Ram Das paused at the door of his house before going in. Two hours to noon, yet the summer sun was fierce. The hot wind, whipping dust from a deserted roadway, would blow mercilessly for six or seven hours yet. No sensible person would go out now until evening, until the shadow of that nearby tree lengthened and came round across the courtyard.

He glanced across at the tree, its tiny new leaves a miracle that amazed him every year. Two wells in the village were completely dry. The third had only a few feet of water left. The river was merely a rocky bed. Yet this startling green freshness had appeared yesterday and would remain for a day or two until dust coated each new leaf, as it coated every single thing in this season of scorching heat. Moisture there must be somewhere, but too deep to be of use to man or beast.

Too deep to be of use ..... too deep to be of use. As he went inside to pass the next few hours in the comparative coolness of his dark inner room, Ram Das turned the thought over in his mind ..... too deep to be of use .....

How much of Mother India's rich religious tradition was just that? Here he was, a priest like his father and grandfather before him, versed more than most village priests in Hindu mythology and lore; supposed to guide the ignorant through every conceivable event, expected or unexpected, in the life of their present incarnation and beyond; revered by all, trusted by most, loved by some; but how tiny a fraction of knowledge was his! He loved the rhythm of the "Bhagavadgita" and other scriptures. He enjoyed the sense of mystery bred by chanting parts of them at times of worship, and he knew the prestige value of such incantations in the opinion of the villagers. Yet what did he understand of God? This ultimate aim of losing one's identity in the Supreme Being – had he advanced one step towards it?

Too hot to sleep, he lay restless on the mud floor, restless not only in body but in soul, and let his thoughts wander back over the years.

* * *

The little lad was puzzled. He was happy here at home, yet Father said that tomorrow he would take him to the town some miles away. Then he'd have to go every day with the older boys of their village. Yes, school-days had come.

*True, the school building was big only in comparison with houses in his village, but to Ram Das it seemed enormous, especially the high-roofed assembly hall in the centre. The four class-rooms, two at either end, were friendlier. Gradually people became friendlier too, and Jyoti was soon his special chum. Jyoti's home was just across the road. He hadn't to walk three miles to school every day! The fact that he hadn't a real mother or father of his own didn't seem to bother him. He belonged to a family all the same. And he took care to let Ram Das know that really it was **his** school they attended!*

Slowly the sound of numbers became familiar. Marks on blackboard and slate took on meaning. Songs and stories told of a God who loves and cares, who saves us from sin if we believe on him. And so five years passed. Only when he moved on to another school did he realise that in Jyoti's there had been a different atmosphere – of reverence and happiness.

* * *

Ram Das arrived home from school one evening to find confusion everywhere. An hour before, Father had been up in a tree cutting wood, missed his footing, and crashed to the ground. At once the priest was called from the next village and was now beside the critically ill man, burning incense, chanting mantras, *trying to release him from the power that made him so pale and helpless. But to no avail. At sundown, in the crowded, smoke-filled room, Father died. No shrieking nor agonised wails could recall him.*

As eldest son, Ram Das had the main rôle in elaborate funeral ceremonies and in the sad procession down to the Burning Ghat by the river next morning. He and other relatives did their very best to ensure a good future for the departed one. But it was all so uncertain!

Now Ram Das was village priest. His young bride, betrothed years ago, was now brought home, and under his mother's watchful eye began to learn her many duties. There were his two younger brothers and three sisters to look after – the lads to be educated, the girls' marriages to arrange. It all cost money. Rupees in the tin trunk – kept in a recess specially built into the inner wall of the house – were not many, but would help keep away the bogey of debt until Ram Das's income from temple duties began to grow.

* * *

The rains had come in earnest when their first child was born – only a girl, but a sweet little thing when cleaned from the grime of being born on a mud floor. Oh, the fear that gripped that young mother's heart when, a few days later, she refused to feed! Mercilessly the dread disease of tetanus took over, choking, starving, convulsing the tiny infant. Two days later wailing from bereaved hearts again rent the air.

The next time a baby was expected the young wife took care to observe all precautions possible, doing exactly as her mother-in-law and husband told her. Such rejoicing when a son was born! He would be named after the good sun, Suraj.

Another year's rains came and went; not good rains – late to come, early to go and scanty all along. The rice crop came to nothing. The millet harvest was light. Every family guarded jealously what little rice and wheat it had, eking them out with coarser grains and stunted vegetables. Prices soared. Then, mercifully, the winter rains were on time. The wheat crop was safe. God be praised! The priest, whose attention to the idols in his care must have saved them from worse famine, was not forgotten.

* * *

Thin cotton clothes are scant protection against cold winds night and morning, especially for a body weakened by poor diet. When little Suraj's cough went on to high fever and laboured breathing, Ram Das decided that his own remedies were not enough. After all, a **son's** illness deserved full attention! The family made its way along the rough road to town, and so to hospital. Ram Das remembered having treatment here as a boy when cut in a fight at school. He knew to sit outside while someone sang and preached. But this time his ears were tuned only to the voice from inside, calling patients by turn. At last, registered, examined, and treated, with his injection stinging like a wasp, Suraj found refuge in the folds of his mother's sari. No, they can't possibly stay in hospital. Suraj's father will bring them tomorrow. Yes, he'll bring money for another injection.

And so for four days the little group swelled numbers at the dispensary. As the illness lost its hold and danger receded Ram Das felt the doctor's interest wane, but the nurse's attention was as concerned and loving as ever. Yes, there was here, as there had been in Jyoti's school, a feeling that people **care**. Perhaps he would read again his prize books from far-away school-days, or this booklet the preacher gave today. This person they talked about, Jesus – his claim to be the **only** way to God was surely extreme. Still, in his name prayer had been made for Suraj, and now Suraj was well again.

* * *

What! Tents going up near our village? Yes, over there, under the banyan tree. Who are coming? The Agricultural Development people? No, the Christian folk, Indians and foreigners. Yes, and they'll be having special meetings for children too, Suraj told his mother excitedly.

Weeks passed. The villagers treated the campers with great kindness and became genuine friends. Medicines were welcome. The little children in camp were a great attraction – each one an orphan like Jyoti had been, all of different castes, but now one happy family. Fancy a member of that proud caste, guardians of the sacred cow, playing, sleeping, and even eating with a child of leather workers! And drinking water brought by a lad born in a Muslim home! Very strange!

Ram Das listened with a smile as Suraj and his small sister recited what they had learned in the tent. Jesus was born – there was no room in the inn – he's knocking at our heart's door today – is there room? Jesus is the water of life and whoever drinks of that water will never thirst again.

* * *

Stirring from his drowsy reminiscing, Ram Das rolled over to a cooler patch on the floor. Funny that those people hadn't been back to visit recently! He had met one of them in town some weeks ago. She had smiled, said they'd love to come back, but were far too busy just then. Well, why couldn't some of the **men** *come? After all, men prefer talking to men! And that fellow-Indian had talked so earnestly! He had spoken about Jesus in such a way that you'd think he wanted you to follow him only! Ram Das couldn't remember all that he had said. But was sin much more than breaking caste rules? Was salvation different from escaping from the cycle of death and rebirth? Did it not depend on good works? In the depths of his heart the priest had begun to doubt.*

But what did those foreigners – or even the Indian Christians who had never known Hinduism as the very fabric of life – what did they know of what it would mean for him to break with the old faith? His whole livelihood, that of his ageing mother, brothers and sisters, his own wife and children – he glanced at them lying asleep across the room – all depended on his priesthood. Not only that (he could possibly find other employment), but not one single person in this whole village, not one other living person in his close acquaintance would take anything more to do with him if they heard of such a thing, unless in a desperate attempt to reclaim him. The price was very high.

And yet, water for soul drought would be priceless. Even knowing that its freshness was temporary, he envied the tree across the courtyard its hidden sources. But of what real use was that water when neither grass nor grain, man nor beast could benefit from it? That was no picture of a Saviour! Suraj's song of the Water of Life – what did it mean? Did no Christian care at all to come and tell them more?

I ABOUT THE HEART

'Let the hearts of those who seek the Lord rejoice.' [Psa. 105.3]

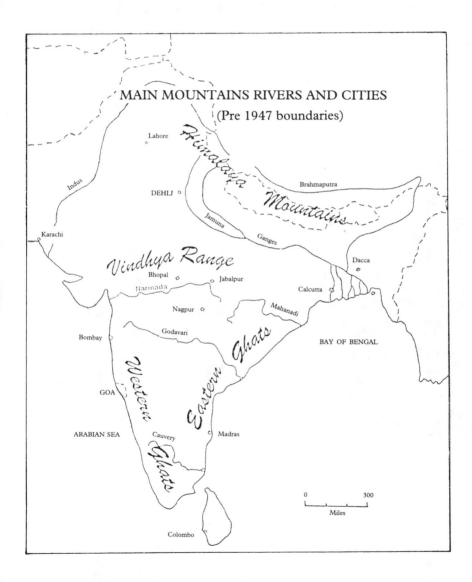

MAIN MOUNTAINS RIVERS AND CITIES
(Pre 1947 boundaries)

1
India – Place and People

The area of Madhya Pradesh in which the Free Church of Scotland has had a particular interest during the twentieth century is in the centre of India. A thousand miles to the north lie the Himalayas ("the abode of snow"). Stretching from Afghanistan to south-west China, this mighty mountain range forms the country's northern frontier. Pakistan to the west, Bangladesh and Burma to the east, and Sri Lanka in the ocean not far from its southern tip are India's close neighbours. Events on any of its borders may have disturbing repercussions, while sectarian rivalries within India itself are a constant threat to peace.

There has been repeated interference from outside. Time after time, intruders have come round one or other end of the Himalayan range. Western nations, on the other hand, arrived by sea. Because of the sheer size of the country, the central part has experienced only the backwash of these successive waves of invasion. Here are found the sturdy, humorous people of the Gondh tribes. They belong to one of the *Adivasi* groups, "the original inhabitants" of the subcontinent.

From about 2500-1500 B.C. the Indus Valley civilisation flourished. Archaeology gives evidence of an advanced society based on highly organised agriculture supplemented by active commerce. This civilisation is believed to have collapsed in the sixteenth century B.C. when Aryans from Central Asia invaded the valley of the Indus River. Water being all-important, the Indus gave its name to the whole subcontinent. The Aryans, taking their Hindu religion with them and intermarrying as they went, spread first to the Punjab ("the land of five rivers"), then eastwards, right along the fertile plain of the Ganges River. Some penetrated slowly south across the Vindhya Hills into peninsular India.

The area in which we are most interested is part of this central tableland, some two thousand feet above sea level. Scrub covers the low, flat-topped hills where teak is grown as a commercial crop. Although these trees are not massive as in a wetter climate, the Hindi word *jungle* describes such territory. Intervening tracts of agricultural land are of rather poor quality, now much improved by irrigation. There, near Lakhnadon, is the country's watershed. The river Bijana joins the Wainganga, which flows by Chhapara eastwards into the Godavari, and so to the Bay of Bengal. The Sher Nadi ("the tiger river") flows under the Jabalpur road about eight miles north of Lakhnadon, then joins the Narmada river, that runs westwards into the Arabian Sea.

India's central tableland drops to the sea on either side by *ghats,* a word that suggests the steps of a ladder. Unlike those on the east, the Western Ghats are rugged and first rise to four thousand feet before descending to sea level. This has a double significance. They break the monsoon clouds coming in off the ocean, and so the area is watered. Also, during the time of Muslim supremacy they were a fortress for guerilla warriors of the Maratha race.

Having looked at the terrain, we now consider the people living there. The Gondhs are an important group in the area where the Free Church of Central India now is. Even before Aryans and Muslims invaded from the north, Gondh kings were powerful. They lived in huge forts impressive even in ruins today. Their religion – Animism – was characterised by the worship of spirits believed to inhabit trees, rivers and rocks, but has become syncretised with Hinduism over many centuries. These people still fear repercussions from the anger of a deity should they abandon traditional ways of worship.

Several different periods may be traced in the early history of India. From 1500 B.C. for 2,500 years, the Aryans (Hindus) were supreme, especially in the north. Muslim armies from farther north were raiding India by the tenth century A.D. This led to the establishment of small Muslim kingdoms, which were absorbed in the Muslim Mogul Empire established in 1526. The eighteenth century was one of fragmented government, followed by British supremacy from about 1800 until 1947. From that time India has prided herself on being a secular democracy.

During the Hindu period, beginning with the Aryan invasions, significant writings appeared. While not historical in the Western sense, they embody an immense volume of philosophical thought.

The "Rig Veda" is an ancient collection of hymns, reverencing sun, storms and sky. The "Upanishads" teach that an individual soul must strive to escape from itself and be merged in the world soul, of which it is a part. The twin doctrines of *karma* (action and its inevitable results) and of transmigration or re-incarnation (the continuing existence of one soul in body after body after body, of whatever kind) originated here. The writings called "Vendanta" ("the goal of the Veda") develop the idea of *maya* or illusion. They teach that man's ultimate goal should be to rid himself of all desire, break links with the physical, and so lose himself in Ultimate Reality.

The "Brahmanas" take their name from Brahma, the first of Hinduism's three main gods. He is seen as the Creator, and from different parts of his body the different Hindu castes are said to have originated. Many are the stories of Vishnu, the preserver god, and of Shiv, the destroyer; or rather of their *"avatar"*, their many appearances to man. Followers of Shiv are distinguished by the mark of a trident, and ash, on their foreheads. More homage is given to Shiv's blood-thirsty wife, Kali or Durga. Vishnu's most popular appearances are Ram and Krishna. As Ram he is the celebrated hero of an epic poem, the "Ramayan". As Krishna he is depicted in the guise of an amorous cowherd in the great "Mahabharat" legend. These names linked with the word *hari* – a name for god – have become familiar in the West. The monotonous chant of "Hari Krishna, Hari Ram" can be heard on city streets in many parts of Britain. Common greetings in the villages of Central India are "Jai Ram" ("victory to Ram") and "Sita Ram", Sita being Ram's exemplary wife.

A third appearance of Vishnu is Jagannath, "lord of the world". The word is carried over into English as the "juggernaut" of our motorways. Less sophisticated than other idols, Jagannath's simple outline is reminiscent of the stones and wooden posts that the animistic Gondh people use to indicate their reverence for the spirit world. This similarity may well illustrate Hinduism's genius for absorption of other traditions. Hinduism – tolerant of all but intolerance – has many branches. All have in common the caste system in which Brahmans are supreme; veneration of the cow; belief in *karma;* and belief in reincarnation.

Buddhism originated in India in the sixth century B.C., and two hundred years later the great Aryan ruler Ashok became a Buddhist. It is now represented in Madhya Pradesh by Tibetans, refugees from the time when China invaded their country in the 1950s. The founder of Buddhism, Gautama Buddha, advocated the stifling of all desire. This, together with compassion for other creatures, should lead to *nirvana* ("extinction"). Buddhism tends towards atheism. So does the Jain religion, of similar antiquity. Jain temples are prominent landmarks in Chhapara, Lakhnadon, Seoni and Jabalpur. Jains stress non-violence. Early missionaries in Chhapara were advised not to throw out egg-shells, evidence of the destruction of potential life, since that would offend Jain neighbours. Successful in business, particularly with textiles, Jain merchants are prominent members of society in the towns of Central India.

The Sikh religion began in the fifteenth century A.D. as a reform movement within Hinduism, but now considers itself quite separate. Its followers reject caste and idolatry, and stress the unity of humanity. They are traditionally good soldiers. Suspicion that Sikhs in Britain and Canada now finance unrest in the Punjab is responsible, in part, for India's current visa restrictions.

Muslims now form 11% of India's population. The founder of Islam, Muhammad, who lived early in the seventh century A.D., claimed to receive from God (Allah) direct revelation which, committed to writing, is the Quran. Pilgrimage to his birthplace of Mecca and burial place of Medina (both in Saudi Arabia); regard for the Quran; regular prayer times; giving to the poor; and fasting in the month of Ramadan are the five pillars of this religion. Strong in its insistence on the equality of all men, but weak in its lack of forgiveness by means of sacrificial love, Islam expects to spread, by coercion as well as persuasion.

The conversion to Islam of nomadic races in Central Asia added the impetus of religious zeal to their naturally adventurous spirit. From 1000 A.D. for five hundred years, Arabs, Afghans, Mongols and Turks came sweeping into India. For two hundred years from the founding of the great Mogul Empire by Babar in 1526 North India had comparative peace. Mogul emperors were men of fine education. They loved architectural beauty (witness the Taj Mahal), and were even tolerant to people of other faiths. Then came Aurangzeb. Fanatically faithful to Muhammad, he was determined to exterminate Hinduism and to take over the government of Central India from Muslim kings who were lax in their loyalty to Islam. Chaos resulted, since his armed forces were part Muslim, part Rajput – a proud remnant of Aryan (Hindu) stock. Maratha fighters, hating Aurangzeb for his intolerance, came out of their highland fortresses in the Vindhya Hills to take advantage of the confusion.

After Aurangzeb's death in 1707, the Mogul Empire disintegrated. The Marathas did well for about fifty years, especially in Central India. But their ambition to govern the whole country was thwarted in 1761 by the Afghans, who had swooped down from Kabul to take possession of Delhi. Muslims in North and Central India began to reassert their authority in local government. Seoni was founded by Muhammad Amin Khan in 1774 when he moved his centre there from Chhapara.

By that time, the British were powerful in India. Back in 1600 some London merchants had banded together for trade with the East Indies, forming the East India Company. Mogul emperors allowed them to establish coastal trading stations. The British outstripped their European rivals because of superior naval support. To protect itself against attack, the Company formed its own army, recruiting local men into its ranks. In the

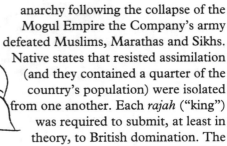

anarchy following the collapse of the Mogul Empire the Company's army defeated Muslims, Marathas and Sikhs. Native states that resisted assimilation (and they contained a quarter of the country's population) were isolated from one another. Each *rajah* ("king") was required to submit, at least in theory, to British domination. The trading corporation had developed into a form of government, and by about 1800 it was the strongest force in the land. The Company even appointed the Governor-General of India, although he was subject to Parliament in London.

It is not surprising that discontent smouldered among Indian troops under British officers in the army of this foreign power. Mutiny erupted in 1857, making it clear that the East India Company was not a competent organ of government. The British Parliament took over direct control. A vast network of railways and canals was built, allowing quick transport of food in times of famine. Facilities for health and education improved. The Civil Service mushroomed, giving employment to thousands.

But many nationals, taking advantage of good education, experienced only frustration, all higher administrative posts being held by colonials. The Indian National Congress was therefore formed in 1885. Slowly but surely it worked for political reform, and, on 15th August 1947, India became independent. However, the vision which the popular leader Mahatma Gandhi had of a subcontinent where people of different religious faiths could live peacefully together was shattered. The Muslim leader Muhammad Ali Jinnah insisted on a separate Islamic state. Partition, resulting in the formation of Pakistan and today's India, coincided with Independence. It was marred by intercommunal violence.

Pakistan today consists of what was West Pakistan then. East Pakistan, separated from the western part by the mass of North India, broke free in 1971 to form Bangladesh. Mahatma Gandhi was assassinated in 1948 by a fellow-Hindu who grudged concessions made to non-Hindus. Jawaharlal Nehru led the Congress Party in government until his death in 1964. His successor, Lal Bahadur Shastri, died after only two years as Prime Minister and was followed in that office by Nehru's daughter, Mrs Indira Gandhi. Government practices during a time of Emergency were so unpopular that a coalition of opposition parties, mainly Hindu, was in power from 1977 for two and a half years, with Moraji Desai as Prime Minister.

Their performance was not impressive and Mrs Gandhi made a come-back as Prime Minister until shot dead by two members of her Sikh bodyguard in 1984. The assassination is reckoned to have been instigated by Sikh extremists, agitating for a separate state in the Punjab. Earlier in 1984 they had been incensed when government troops entered their most holy shrine, the Golden Temple at Amritsar, where armed men were hiding. Mrs Gandhi's son, Rajiv, then held office as Prime Minister until 1989.

Since Independence the country has fraternised with Russia. How India may yet change in response to the increasing openness now in the Communist world remains to be seen. Her claim to be a secular socialist democratic republic does not prevent bitter intercommunal and inter-regional discord even now. The strongest of human leaders would be hard-pressed to hold together all the pieces of the vast and vigorous jigsaw that is India.

Wonderful place! Wonderful people!

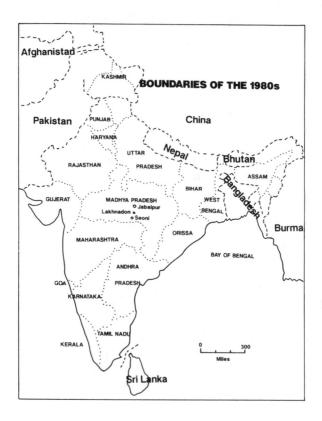

a sound to remember

In January 1975, Kathleen Macleod and I spent a week in an isolated village a few miles beyond Adegaon. Concerned about the number of people there with tuberculosis, we did a house-to-house survey.

At noon on the Lord's Day a man came, asking us to go and treat an ill child at his home. We went on foot. Warm sunshine drew a sweet scent from huge, crackly teak leaves covering the ground. After a mile or two the path led down to a river, easy to cross in winter, along fields green with young wheat, and up to his village. Passing a tiny temple, we heard the loud voice of a priest intoning Hindu scriptures.

*The infant, ill with pneumonia, would soon respond to the injection of penicillin. (What **did** our seniors do without antibiotics?) Over a cup of tea we spoke of Jesus – an unfamiliar name there – and gave out some gospel portions. Then our guide warned that tigers would be on the prowl after sunset.*

When we left the village the same strong voice of the priest was intoning in Hindi, from one of our booklets, the opening verses of John's Gospel. A sound to remember. As far as I know, no Christian had gone to that place before, nor has any visited it since.

It was cool as we walked back through the beautiful bare jungle.

In 1989 I still wonder if the priest has ever understood what he was reading.

2
India Hears of Christ

Gondh tribal people, Hindus, Muslims, Buddhists, Jains, Sikhs – these have been mentioned already. What about Christians in India? Who are they, and how have they come to faith in Jesus?

Ask almost any Indian Christian today about the origins of the church in his land and Thomas will be mentioned. There is a strong tradition in South India that the Apostle Thomas came to Kerala in 52 A.D., arousing interest in Christ among some Brahman families; that he moved on to Singapore and China; and later returned to Madras where he was killed by hostile Brahmans in 72 A.D. The earliest writings in support of this are from 250 A.D. It is known that during the first century sea-trade between the Roman Empire and India was established, the strong south-west and gentler north-east monsoon winds filling the merchant-ships' sails. Roman coins of that time have been found along the south-west coast of the subcontinent. So it is possible that Thomas did begin to evangelise India. The tradition remains strong.

Archaeology gives evidence of a community of Christians in South India around 800 A.D. Five copper plates, written in the old Tamil script but with signatures in a variety of Persian, Arabic and Hebrew characters, record certain privileges and responsibilities given to Christians by a local king. They were evidently foreigners settled in India with pastors sent from Persia. To this day, Syrian Christians are a distinct group in South India. The original element is now well diluted with local blood yet still proud of roots in Syria, Mesopotamia and Persia.

After Muhammad established Islam in the seventh century A.D., his followers conquered Persia. They gained control over the oceans and so broke links between East and West, links not to be restored for about seven hundred years. By 1300, the Mongols of Central Asia, who had turned Muslim, opposed Christianity fiercely. The church in those parts was persecuted and almost obliterated. Far away in South India, it survived.

Marco Polo of Italy passed through India *en route* to and from China, probably in 1288 and 1292. He records the industry of Christians in cultivating coconuts and he relates legends about the shrine of Thomas near Madras. Through Vasco da Gama, Portugal wrested control of the Indian Ocean from the Arabs, maintaining control from 1500 for 150 years. Goa, south of Bombay, became and still is a Roman Catholic stronghold. In 1542, Francis Xavier, Jesuit missionary and special ambassador of the King of Portugal, arrived. Although he spent only four years in India before going on to Japan, his influence there was great. Having organised church life in Goa, he travelled widely along the Coromandal coast south of Madras among a fisher caste, the Paravas. Anxious to have protection by the Portuguese authorities against raiders, the Paravas moved as a body of about ten thousand people into the Roman Catholic fold. Jesuit leaders worked hard to absorb the Syrian "Thomas" church. They succeeded, apparently, just as the sixteenth century ended. Fifty years later, however, there was a secession. The Thomas church was reconstituted. Denying the dominion of Rome, it clings to its ancient Eastern traditions.

The Mogul emperor Akbar (1556-1605), ruling in North India, showed an interest in Christianity as an alternative to Islam and invited Jesuits from Goa to his court. Although Akbar's successor Jehangir allowed three of his nephews to be baptised, little headway was made and later rulers quashed the venture.

Back in the South, an Italian Jesuit, Roberto Nobili, laboured during the first half of the seventeenth century. Indianising his life-style and teaching, he adopted some Brahman practices and allowed high-caste persons to retain some Hindu customs after baptism. As a result, the maintenance of caste distinctions is still a serious obstacle in church life there today. Nobili had two successors. One was beheaded by a local ruler after twenty years of lonely witness. The other distinguished himself by excellence in the Tamil language – and by his fierce opposition to Protestant Lutheran missionaries who arrived in 1706.

Protestant influence in India began through chaplains of trading corporations. The British East India Company discouraged evangelism as something likely to alienate its Indian patrons. Danish trading posts were set up in 1620 at Tranquebar in Madras State and at Serampore, fifteen miles upstream from Calcutta. In 1676, King Frederick IV, an earnest Christian, established the Royal Danish Mission at his own expense. No Danes volunteered but two German Lutheran pietists, Ziegenbalg and Pluetschau, were recruited. Ordained in Denmark, they arrived in Tranquebar in 1706. They met with a hostile reception from both European merchants and Indians. Setting themselves to learn Tamil as well as Portuguese (the language of trade), they gave priority to translating the Bible and to establishing schools and orphanages. How to print the Word was a problem. This need was made known by a chaplain in the British royal house as Queen Anne, who was then on the British throne, was married to a Dane. And so a London-based organisation, the Society for Promoting Christian Knowledge (S.P.C.K.), gave a printing-press to the Tranquebar Mission.

In South India, an outstanding character of the second half of the eighteenth century was the German missionary Schwartz. A humble servant of God, he was influential in many spheres. At home with high and low, this "royal priest of Tanjore" gathered in a Christian flock of about twenty thousand during his forty-eight years' service.

Evangelism farther south near Cape Comorin, the Land's End of India, resulted in a mass movement among the Hadars, traditional harvesters of the sweet juice of palmyra palms. Over five thousand were baptised in the period 1800-1803. A faithful Indian pastor, Satyanathan, along with German, Welsh and English men of God, was used to establish them in the faith.

Charles Grant of Glenurquhart, a member of the Council of Bengal and later a director of the East India Company, was one of the first to challenge the Company's resistance to Christian missions. The Company's charter was presented to Parliament in London for renewal every twenty years. In 1793 Charles Grant and William Wilberforce proposed a clause directing the Company to send out Christian missionaries. Although this proposal was not accepted, the seed had been sown. In 1813 some concessions were made. Two decades later the doors were wide open.

The Evangelical Revival in England resulted in the birth of many foreign missionary organisations at the end of the eighteenth century. The first such was the Baptist Missionary Society founded in 1792. The cobbler-pastor William Carey (1761-1834) was a founder-member. He was the first Protestant missionary to be sent from Britain. Landing at Calcutta from a Danish ship in 1793 with his wife and four children, he had many hardships to face. His colleague Dr John Thomas was not a competent manager of their joint finances. Soon the group was in dire straits. Thomas, who had previously worked in Bengal, contacted a friendly official who secured posts for both men as managers of indigo dye factories. During five years in that situation, Carey learned Sanskrit and Bengali and was soon translating and teaching God's Word. But still the British authorities were opposed to missionary work.

When more recruits arrived, they were welcomed at the small Danish settlement at Serampore, a haven from the opposition of British officials. Holding to the principle of financial self-sufficiency, Carey was able, by hard work and careful management, to buy land at Serampore. With two faithful colleagues, Marshman, a teacher, and Ward, a printer, he established a Christian community there. Translation, production and distribution of the Scriptures in many Eastern languages went hand in hand with evangelism, education and Dr Thomas's medical services. That devout man of God and brilliant scholar Henry Martyn was influenced at Cambridge by Charles Simeon, and came to India as a chaplain with the East India Company in 1805. He spent part of his seven years' missionary service cooperating with Carey in Bible translation and gave readers of Urdu and Persian fine translations of the New Testament. He died in 1812, aged thirty-one.

In 1800 – the very first year of the Baptist Mission at Serampore – a Hindu carpenter became interested in the Christian faith when Dr Thomas treated his dislocated arm. He believed in Jesus and was baptised. His wife, her sister and a neighbouring family soon followed him; then others from different backgrounds. A Brahman convert married the carpenter's daughter. Definite rejection of caste distinctions proved a source of strength to the church there, in contrast to some groups in South India. Carey and his colleagues emphasised personal faith in Christ, study of God's Word, and prayer.

Carey, Marshman and Ward had a large degree of autonomy and this led to misunderstandings with the Baptist Missionary Society's home committee in England. Despite this, the trio went on to found Serampore College in 1818. Carey's flair for languages led to his being appointed as a professor at the Governor-General's College for junior officials of the East India Company. The salary, which was generous, went into the common purse. Serampore College went from strength to strength for sixty years but towards the end of the century it declined. In 1910 it was resuscitated. Its Arts and Science faculties were then affiliated to Calcutta University while the Theological Department's Senate began to draw members from other Christian bodies. Since 1910, affiliation to Serampore has enabled over forty seminaries in many parts of India to grant degrees.

These seminaries came into being through the work of the many other missionary societies that had sprung up towards the end of the eighteenth century and the beginning of the nineteenth: Anglican, Methodist and Congregational. Restrictions on the entry of non-British missionary organisations were removed when the East India Company's charter was revised in 1833.

The General Assembly of the Church of Scotland decided in 1824 to begin educational work in India. Six months earlier, Thomas Chalmers had been installed as Professor of Moral Philosophy at the University of St Andrews. Among students influenced by him at that time was Alexander Duff of Moulin, Perthshire. After the death of a friend and fellow-student who had intended to be a missionary, Duff, encouraged by his parents, prepared to go instead. With his wife he sailed for Calcutta on 14th October 1829. They arrived six months and two shipwrecks later. (The length of sea voyages accounts for apparent discrepancies in dates. Travellers leaving Scotland in the last quarter of the year would arrive at Bombay in the New Year.) Before Duff left India finally in 1863, he had pioneered education in English and local languages among boys of Calcutta's upper social strata where dissatisfaction with traditional Hinduism had already prepared the ground for Christianity. Although Duff saw fewer than forty of his pupils profess faith in Christ, the impact of his work was enormous - and in other continents as well as in Asia. In India, John Wilson at Bombay, John Anderson at Madras, Thomas Hunter in the Punjab and Stephen Hislop at Nagpur were Scots, contemporary with Duff, and were, like him, pioneers in Christian education. John MacDonald, son of Dr John MacDonald of Ferintosh, "The Apostle of the North", went to Calcutta in 1837, labouring until his death there ten years later. He married an Indian lady. Some of their descendants have strengthened the local church.

Missionary activity increased greatly during the nineteenth century. As a result of practical concern shown for poor people in time of famine, there were sometimes movements of whole communities into the Christian church. When conversion was in name only, the church, although numerically strong, was prone to be spiritually weak. This tendency persists even today.

The organisation of the visible church was taken on largely by foreigners. The usual pattern was to start village schools, whose Indian teachers were trained as catechists. Some took on still more responsibility. In South India a Welshman, John Thomas, led his group of six men on to ordination and full ministry in 1851. In the North, Indian men who had become Christians through the work of Alexander Duff gave leadership in the church.

It was recognised that higher educational standards were desirable. After secondary schools, colleges (including theological seminaries) developed. During the second half of the nineteenth century, the climate of opinion in India was favourable for Christian missions. Some prominent men of good education recognised Christ's claims as paramount and left other faiths to be baptised. Their influence was great. But, in the West, theological liberalism was weakening the churches. Duff had intended his Bible-based English-medium scientific education to be like dynamite, the explosion of which would, in due time, destroy systems of belief that were contrary to Christ. That dynamite was effectively dampened by later missionaries who denied the integrity of Scripture. The May 1903 issue of the magazine "Review of Religion" published in Punjab Province congratulated those Christian missionaries who admitted at last that their source of authority was fallible. Now, the publishers said, it was clear that the Quran was supreme. Even today, many Christian centres of higher education have not recovered their original loyalty to Christ.

Another factor working against Christians at the turn of the century was a reform movement in Hinduism. The Arya Samaj, to name only one of several societies, was set up in 1875 to defend and reform traditional Hinduism. A century later it has lost none of its virulence against Christianity.

Particularly after the "Quit India" call to Britain was heeded in 1947, national Christian leaders were more aware of their obligations to be seen as loyal Indian citizens. The Church of South India, formed in 1947 from episcopal and non-episcopal bodies, was reckoned to be a blueprint for union between churches in any continent. The Church of North India, inaugurated at Nagpur in 1970, grew from an earlier Union of 1924, and now includes the majority of churches resulting from the work of mainline Western missions north of Bombay. Those in various churches who were not satisfied with the doctrinal basis of the National Christian Council (affiliated to the World Council of Churches) formed, in 1951, the Evangelical Fellowship of India. Rising costs in institutional work encouraged cooperative efforts. In 1953 plans were made for Union Bible Seminary in Maharashtra, Central India. Located first at Yeotmal, now at Pune, it has a good academic standard. The Free Church considers its doctrinal basis less satisfactory than that of the Presbyterian Theological Seminary at Dehra Dun (formerly at Roorkee) in North India.

The Free Church of Scotland Mission became a member of the Evangelical Fellowship of India (E.F.I.) in 1968. By that time E.F.I. had developed several departments, among others one for Christian Education, set up in 1962, and a Committee on Relief, established in 1967. These have helped Free Church work over the years. The Indian Evangelical

Mission, founded in 1965, is concerned to evangelise millions of people still unreached by Christian witness, especially in rural areas. Their two hundred national missionaries today work in primitive conditions similar to those faced by pioneers from abroad in 1900.

Illiteracy and ignorance of God's Word were not the only challenges to the early pioneers. Disease and destitution (often because of famine and poor agriculture) were also common. Caring for ill people, including particular groups such as sufferers from tuberculosis and leprosy, began in a small way. Carey's companion, Dr John Thomas, was the first qualified medical missionary. In 1819, Dr John Scudder came from America to South India. One of his descendants, Dr Ida Scudder, founded a hospital for women at Vellore, west of Madras. A similar institution was established at Ludhiana in the Punjab in 1894. Both of these have developed into famous Christian Medical Colleges, training men and women in a wide range of medical and para-medical disciplines.

Caste-conscious Hindu people consider nursing a degrading occupation. Hence the majority of India's nurses are of Christian background. Because a doctor's work is considered prestigious as well as remunerative, Indian doctors far outnumber nurses. Throughout the land, but especially in rural areas, Christian hospitals, not least those of the Emmanuel Hospital Association, contribute much to curative and preventative medical care. Since the 1970s, community health and development projects have become widely accepted.

Improved methods of agriculture have been fostered by missionaries from early times. And gradually Westerners have learned to listen to local wisdom: a tractor may be less suitable than a pair of bullocks if the land to be ploughed is a thin layer of top-soil! At Lakhnadon it was hoped that efficient cultivation of the field beside the hospital would help finance Community Health work. Although this hope has not yet been realised, the land produces useful crops and gives employment to local people. The Muldoons, who are associated with the Presbyterian Church of Eastern Australia, have worked at Allahabad's Agricultural Institute since 1982. The lively Christian witness of believers there at the "Ag. Inst." is a bright spot in a rather drowsy part of the Church of North India. Fascinating accounts could be given of many other Christian institutions throughout the country. However, we must move on.

blind but seeing

This story of two orphan children was told by Mrs Anna Thomson (née Stewart) in 1987. The story began in early 1940, when the other missionaries were away at camp and she was on her own in Chhapara for a few weeks.

One morning a little procession approached the bungalow, headed by a villager carrying a young child whom he dumped on the ground. He said the child was blind, its mother dead, and he had to work in the fields all day. He wanted the Mission to accept the child. I think our cook Charan came out to see what was going on and to give me good advice. The father concluded that his gift was accepted, and departed with his friends, leaving the child Chandami on the ground. We felt we must keep him until the "bari" ("big") Miss Sahib returned. We would ask the ayah who looked after Jaiwanti, Prakash and Peter to take him also. He was a poor little specimen, undernourished and none too clean, blind and, apparently, lame. Probably his father didn't think he'd be much of a wage-earner. We handed him over to the ayah.

I was busy and did not see him until late next day. What a transformation! He had been washed and scrubbed, given clean clothes and fed. He was not lame at all, and, though blind, seemed to have a faint glimmer of light in one eye.

Well, the ladies returned from camp and found the new arrival. About the same time the Macleods came in from their camp and called at Chhapara, bringing with them – a little blind girl! They had found Kamala, also motherless, shut up in a hut every day while her father worked in the fields. Gladly he accepted Mr Macleod's offer to take the child to Lakhnadon hospital. (I never heard whose initial suggestion it was.)

After discussion, the missionaries decided that both children must be sent to a Blind School. I think the only one we knew was the Sharp Memorial School for the Blind, at Rajpur, Dehra Dun District, run by the Zenana Bible Medical Mission (later B.M.M.F.). That was on the winding road up to Mussoorie and Landour, where the Missionary Language School was held. I had been there in 1939 and hoped to return for the second year Hindi course. I was deputed to write to Miss Youngs, the Superintendent, to see if our blind children might be accepted. The reply was favourable and I could take them in May. Cyril Thomson, to whom I was engaged, was also going and we planned to join forces for the long train journey with its many changes. The intervening weeks were not wasted. Our two were being brought up with the Christian children, hearing Bible stories and learning to sing psalms and choruses; and were encouraged to trust the Lord Jesus.

The journey to Rajpur began on 1st May 1940 and we arrived on the 4th after several changes of train – Jabalpur to Allahabad, then to Lucknow; after a restful day there at the Kinnaird Hospital, our last train, to Dehra Dun. The night train to Dehra Dun was crammed with pilgrims going to Haridwar, a Hindu holy place. Even the floor at our feet was filled. The children were very good and attracted attention when we were all sleepless, by lifting up their voices and singing a Hindi chorus, "I have begun to follow Jesus. No turning back." Perhaps it was this that aroused in one man an anti-Christian reaction. He was in charge of the party of pilgrims and began to object loudly to our presence in the overcrowded compartment and to Christianity in general. To our surprise, another man came to our defence. "Look at you," he said, "well paid by your pilgrims. These missionaries are caring for blind children. Would you do that, and care for blind people who can't pay you anything?" There was muttered support and the first man subsided. In a few hours, we reached Haridwar and the pilgrims left us. We had room to stretch out and the children had a good sleep. At Dehra Dun, after breakfast and a wash, we took a bus and then a rickshaw, and reached the Blind School. We said goodbye to the children, who had been so good, and handed them over to Miss Youngs.

During the next few years we kept in touch and saw the children from time to time. Miss Youngs told us that an eye-specialist had operated on Chandami's "good" eye and improved the glimmer of light there. Kamala had asked wistfully if she too could have an operation – alas, both eyes were completely dead. On one visit we heard both children singing, "Up from the grave He arose"; and also found that Chandami could play the piano.

The years went by and our paths diverged. We heard nothing about Chandami, but we had an affectionate letter from Kamala in Braille, which a blind friend read to us.

It was in 1984 that a Free Church missionary at Chhapara wrote to suggest that the blind orphans' story might interest readers of "From the Frontiers". What story? For me it had ended forty years earlier. If there was a story I ought to try to trace Chandami. But how? Miss Youngs had long since passed away. I tried without success to tap a few possible sources. Three years went by.

Then in February 1987 I read in a B.M.M.F. magazine that the Sharp Memorial Home, Rajpur, would celebrate its Centenary on 11th April 1987. The name of the present Superintendent was given – Mr Samuel. At once I wrote to him asking if he had in his archives the names of former residents as far back as 1940. I named our two and mentioned my connection.

Several weeks went by with no reply. And then, on 29th April 1987, I had a great surprise – a typed letter from India, in English, signed by D. Chandami. As I read it I was excited to find that this was indeed our Chandami. He wrote that he and his wife (yes, his wife!) had made the journey to Rajpur for the Centenary celebration. There Mr Samuel had read to him my letter. Chandami was so happy that he took down my address to write me. His letter began: "Greetings to you in the name of our Lord and Saviour ..... Yes, I am in Sharp Memorial School in Rajpur, in which in 1940 you had admitted me from Chhapara. For this I earnestly thank you and our Lord."

He went on to say that he and his wife Mary now work at a Blind School attached to a Swedish Lutheran Mission Hospital in M.P. He has a married son, a photographer; a grandson of two and a half years; and an unmarried daughter who teaches at a Mission School. "We thank God for all His help and guidance. Really He has blessed us."

I was astonished at his news. How had all this come about? Where had he been all the years since 1940? I had not heard from Mr Samuel, but in a few days his letter came. He apologised for the delay, due to Centenary affairs. He enclosed a picture he had taken specially for me of Chandami and his wife, with Kamala. "Kamala," he wrote, "is one of the best blind people I have met so far. She always has a smile, and is extremely cooperative and helpful to others. She remembers you very well and asks me to send you her greetings."

It was the first picture I had ever seen of the two orphans. Chandami was wearing dark glasses. Kamala's hair was quite white. You would not know she was blind. Dear Kamala!

When I wrote Chandami expressing pleasure at all his news, I asked him to fill in for me the forty-odd years of which I knew nothing. Weeks later came a happy reply. In the top corner, he put "Psalm 91: 9-16". Again he began, "Greetings to you in the most precious and loving name of our Lord Jesus Christ." He outlined his career from 1947.

"In 1947, I went to the School for the Blind, St Michael, Ranchi, Bihar, for studies up to Middle School. After clearing the Board examination, I went to Dehra Dun Training Centre for the Blind, and completed the two years' course. I got my first appointment as a teacher, in June 1955, at the School for the Blind at Mungeli, District Bilaspur, M.P., and served there for fifteen years. The school was closed, and I got the appointment as a Braille teacher in Padhar School for the Blind, where I am presently serving. I was married on 15th June 1959 in Mungeli Church. At present, my age is 50 years. In short this is my humble history."

He said that his little grandson, Vincent Anupam, is a great joy to them. He enclosed a family photo in colour, taken during their hot-weather holiday at their son's home.

I have gazed and gazed at this picture, and this good-looking family. I am filled with amazement at God's goodness to a little, motherless blind child. He had had a good education and is a qualified teacher, knowing both Hindi and English. He has the joy of a wife and family. Above all, he has found the Lord *and is a real Christian.*

Missionary work is often discouraging and unrewarding. The strongholds of Hinduism, allied with generations of ignorance, seem impregnable. Who could have foretold that seed sown in the hearts of Chandami and Kamala would bear fruit today?

Chandami in particular could lay claim to this verse – Isaiah 42: 16:

"And I will bring the blind by a way that they know not. I will lead them in paths that they have not known. I will make darkness light before them, and crooked things straight. These things will I do unto them, and not forsake them."

3

Christian Witness in Seoni Area

Visitors to Lakhnadon today usually travel the six hundred miles south from Delhi to Jabalpur by rail or air, and then cover the last fifty-three miles by road.

The first Christian witness probably arrived from the opposite direction – from Nagpur, about 120 miles south of Lakhnadon. Carey had sent an evangelist there from Serampore about 1814. Thirty years later, Stephen Hislop was sent by the Free Church of Scotland. At the Disruption in 1843, all but one of the overseas missionaries of the Church of Scotland decided to join the Free Church of Scotland. Spiritual life was vigorous and, in spite of much poverty, money was given sacrificially for home and foreign missions.

Hislop came from Duns. He believed passionately in education as a preparation for the gospel: Alexander Duff was his model. A keen interest in geology gave him common ground with British army officers, a good number of whom came to faith in Christ through his witness. Perhaps some of them were posted to Seoni after the native state of Nagpur was brought under British rule in 1853. Hislop was drowned in a swollen stream while riding back from a village visit in 1863. He was forty-six years old.

Dissatisfied with the abuse of the system of patronage, the Original Seceders broke from the established Church of Scotland in 1733. Over the next 119 years, there were movements to unite with other bodies, and in 1852 the Free Church received the majority of Original Seceders into its fold.

Those continuing as the Synod of the United Original Seceders (from now on referred to as the Secession) decided in 1868 to raise funds for witness overseas and to look for a sphere where they might be active. The Rev. Dr Murray Mitchell, one of Chalmers' associates at the time of the Disruption, was a Free Church missionary in Western India. In 1870, his visit to a recently-established mission work among Gondh tribal people in Central India was reported in the Secession magazine. It was soon agreed that the Free Church would hand over responsibility for the northern part of its Central Indian field to the Secession.

That agreement was made in 1871, and was followed in the next year by the arrival of the first Secession missionaries. Shortly after his ordination at Glasgow on 22nd August 1871, the Rev. George Anderson, with his wife, left Scotland and sailed, like Duff, round the Cape of Good Hope. Their fares of £40 each were waived by the shipping agents George Smith and Sons. After three and a half months, they arrived at Bombay, where they spent two weeks. They then travelled a night and a day by train the four hundred miles to Nagpur. Free Church missionaries there gave them hospitality for a fortnight. Finally, three days by bullock-wagon on "a very good road" took them the eighty miles to Seoni. There they arrived on 17th January 1872.

By that time, Europeans in the town of Seoni had already built a small Episcopal church. Mr Anderson preached there on Sunday evenings until the following June. An Indian man, converted from Hinduism at the Free Church Institute in Calcutta, was willing to give up his work as head clerk to the British Deputy Commissioner at Seoni, to be an evangelist. Mr Anderson advised his home supporters that this man's salary would be £120 to £130 per annum, plus accommodation. There seems to have been no thought of his being supported locally.

Hostile to missionary work though the British government had sometimes been, officials in Nagpur and Seoni gave good help. Through their cooperation, Mr Anderson was able to buy, for £300, a large house in five acres of ground at the "nice and airy" north end of the town. In the face of fierce opposition from local Muslims, they reported that they felt safe "under the strong arm of British protection".

The Andersons returned to Scotland for health reasons after eighteen years. An Irishman, the Rev. Edward White, joined them in 1881, leaving after only a few years because of his wife's illness. Between 1888 and 1898, Mr Robert Blakely and the Rev. David Finlayson from Scotland worked in Seoni. In 1898, the Rev. John McNeel began his fifty-six years' ministry there.

One of eight in the family of a minister in the Associate Presbyterian Church of North America, John McNeel was born and brought up in

Pittsburgh, Indiana. His father died in 1881, when John was thirteen years old. After graduating B.A. at Geneva College, Beaver Falls, Pennsylvania, he studied at the Original Secession Divinity Hall in Scotland. His home church agreed to join forces with the Secession for work overseas. He was ordained, and set apart for work in Seoni, on 18th November 1897 in Victoria Terrace Church, Edinburgh. (When approaching the Free Church Assembly Hall from Victoria Terrace today, you may notice a very faint sign, "Original Secession Church", pointing to what is now a Quaker Meeting House.)

He and his wife Margaret (née Littlejohn), who came from Perth, then served together for forty-one years in Seoni. Her broad Perthshire accent and unaffected kindliness complemented her husband's brisk efficiency. Young British men in government service at Seoni could banish homesickness in the company of that caring mother and her little ones. The McNeels had five children. The first was still-born and one died in infancy. Mrs McNeel herself died at Seoni in 1938 and was buried there. That same year the second youngest daughter, Mary, returned to Seoni as a missionary nurse. She was companion to her father until his death there in 1954. The Secession joined the Church of Scotland in 1957, and the Seoni work was incorporated into the United Church of North India which in turn became part of the Church of North India in 1970. Mary stayed on at Seoni until retiring to Edinburgh and even now visits friends in India as often as she can.

John McNeel impressed those who knew him by his obvious devotion to the Lord and by the charm of his personality. His energy and practical abilities were amazing. A memorial booklet published by the Secession tells that he was "his own architect, his own clerk of works, his own brick-maker, his own contractor and his own builder. Nothing, in fact, was done except on his advice and under his personal supervision." This was the man with whom Foreign Missions' Committee Conveners in Scotland corresponded regarding the overseas work of the Secession and of the Free Church in the early twentieth century.

In the Union of 1900, a large majority of the Free Church combined with the United Presbyterians to form the United Free Church. The Free Church of Scotland was left as a remnant. All her 166 missionaries – in Budapest, Constantinople, Syria, the New Hebrides, South Arabia, Africa and India – had entered the Union. Yet the Free Church was determined to maintain interest overseas. "The Monthly Record" of March 1901 reported a meeting in Milton Free Church, Glasgow, in support of the Secession work in India. Four months later the magazine told of the arrival at Seoni in January 1901 of Dr Jeannie Grant. Brought up in Glenurquhart Free Church, she was recruited by the Secession for medical and evangelistic work in India. She served there until her death in 1953.

At the turn of the century, waves of famine, cholera, plague and smallpox broke up families throughout India, leaving thousands of orphans. Women and children especially suffered from lack of medical care. Illiteracy was the norm in villages. Christian missions and Hindu reform groups responded to these needs. The Rev. John McNeel was in great demand by British government officials as an organiser of "plague camps" and of relief schemes in connection with famine or epidemics. Dr Jeannie Grant was awarded the prestigious *Kaisar-i-Hind* gold medal by King George VI for her service to Medicine in India. But, however much they were seen as servants of the British Raj, the missionaries were concerned primarily with Gospel witness.

Rev. John McNeel   *Dr. Jeannie Grant*

The missionary pioneer in Seoni, the Rev. George Anderson, had retired in 1890. In 1904 he contributed a series of articles to "The Monthly Record" to inform readers about the area where the Free Church of Scotland had begun to support the Secession work. Part of one article is given here. Although the style is old-fashioned, it gives an accurate picture of the pattern that the Free Church work followed.

All friends of the mission cause are not quite agreed as to the manner in which the work should be prosecuted. Divinely appointed methods ought never to be neglected; but it does not follow that we must pursue only one course whatever the circumstances in which we are placed. In this paper the reader's attention will be called to different branches of work that have received, and still are receiving attention in the Seoni district.

The Preaching of the Gospel is the chief means which Christ intends the Church to use in seeking the conversion of the world. Paul esteemed it a favour to be called to preach among the Gentiles the unsearchable riches of Christ; and those who neglect the preaching of the Cross, whatever success they may attain in other directions, may well be addressed in these words, "These things ye ought to have done and not to leave the other undone".

1. Preaching in English ought in most districts to occupy a very subordinate place. To condemn all such preaching by missionaries is wrong; for our countrymen need the gospel, and in many cases can hear it from no other than from a missionary. Many a one who has left Britain destitute of the saving knowledge of Christ has been saved by the simple, faithful preaching of missionaries; and such persons prove valuable auxiliaries in the work of missions. From the very foundation of the Seoni mission this work has been carried on and good fruit reaped from it.

2. Preaching in the vernacular is indispensable in a district like Seoni. Much preparation is needed for vernacular preaching in connection with the study of the languages, and also in acquiring knowledge of the opinions and practices and modes of thought of the people. In preaching to mixed audiences one has to be very careful to prevent the hearers from misunderstanding the purpose of the discourse; and sometimes it is necessary to warn them against the mistakes they are apt to make. It would be absurd to preach to Muslims against the worship of idols, which they abhor, or to tell Hindus that they must be born again, without explaining that regeneration is entirely different from the heathen doctrine of reincarnation.

    (a) Wherever a church has been founded the gospel must be preached in the vernacular in the regular place of meeting – the church. The character of the preaching must be determined by circumstances, but the aim of the preacher should ever be to edify believers and to convince and turn to God those who are mere professors, and others still heathen who may be present. To preach with the requisite simplicity and pointedness, and at the same time to avoid sameness, is no easy task. Discussion is not generally allowed in church at the ordinary diets of worship.

(b) Preaching in villages and towns is a very important branch of mission work in all rural missions. It is advisable to reach the village which is to be first visited about daybreak, before the people get dispersed among the fields to their daily labour. Often the chief man in the village, called the *patail*, will send someone to gather the people together; sometimes he declines to give any assistance. In this case the missionary must do his best to gather them. He will generally converse with them on some topic of local interest, or about seedtime and harvest, and use such subjects to draw the interest to heavenly and divine things. A portion of Scripture will be read and the teaching of it expounded with as close application to the audience as possible. Discussion is generally allowed and encouraged, unless the opposition to the gospel be evidently disruptive. When the meeting is over, a second village will be visited, and even a third; sometimes a whole day is spent in going from village to village, proclaiming to the benighted inhabitants the good news of the gospel. A tour of a few days is sometimes made among the villages, when the missionary spends the night on the verandah, or in some shed connected with the *patail's* house.

(c) Preaching in markets and fairs is generally much practised in Indian missions. There are three market days in Seoni – Monday, Wednesday and Friday. Controversy is not very desirable in the Seoni markets, as it would often be interminable and vain, but reasonable questions are always answered. In the village markets greater liberty is allowed, as it is not often abused by the simple-minded people who attend them. Thousands of people gather together on the banks of the Wainganga at Chhapara, twenty-one miles to the north of Seoni, in the month of January; and a still larger gathering takes place at the end of October or the beginning of November at a place which is regarded as the source of that river, twelve miles to the south-east of Seoni. These gatherings are called *melas* and have a religious character, but the Hindus know how to combine business with their devotion. In these markets and fairs many people are brought within the hearing of the gospel, whose villages mission agents may not be able to reach.

Educational Work in a private way was begun early in 1872 for the advantage of Eurasian and other Christian children. In January 1876, a Boys' School was opened in the town of Seoni, twenty-two pupils being enrolled on the first day. Before 1889 the number rose to close on three hundred. The school has grown till the building of a schoolhouse to accommodate seven or eight hundred boys has been forced upon us and it is now approaching completion. As it is a High School, Persian and Sanskrit are taught in it, besides Hindi, Hindustani and English. All the children receive daily instruction in the knowledge of the gospel.

No one who duly appreciates the work done by our Scottish Reformers can decry educational work in connection with missions. A splendid opportunity is given in schools, even apart from the Scripture lesson, of pressing home on the young the beauty and value of Christianity, both to the individual and to the community; and the Seoni Mission School has been the means of breaking down the prejudices of many, and of winning for the gospel at least admiration. As in our land, conviction is not always followed by consistent action.

Girls' Schools labour under many disadvantages. Not only is there a widespread prejudice against female education but, even after that prejudice has been overcome, girls are taken from school at a very tender age to be married. The wives of the more respectable natives would not allow their faces to be seen in any public place, even in a school. There are two schools for girls conducted by the Mission in Seoni – one in the mission compound and the other in the town.

Zenana missions have proved of great value in the advancement of Christianity and in the elevation of Indian women. (*Zenana* means a place where men may not enter.) The need for this kind of work in India is very apparent, because native women are not allowed to go freely into society as females are in Scotland. None but females can have free access to them, and *zenana* missions were instituted for the purpose of having the native women taught by European ladies and their native assistants. Various branches are taught according to circumstances, but in all cases the great end aimed at is religious instruction.

It need hardly be said that the **Orphanages**, in which we have over ninety boys and girls, afford specially favourable opportunities for instruction in every branch of education likely to fit them to be good Christians and good citizens. Some of our orphan children have proved very useful in mission work and we hope that many others from among them may be the means of greatly promoting the cause of God in their native land.

Village schools and Sabbath schools are also in operation in different parts of the district and Catechists are employed in out-stations and the villages surrounding them. Thus the work is gradually extending.

Medical Mission Work is the latest and by no means the least important addition to the agencies carried on in Seoni. All along, medicine has been more or less dispensed to the natives in connection with the mission, and with good effect; but only of late years has there been a qualified practitioner among its agents. Good work has been already done by Dr Jeannie Grant. She finds access to many whom no male practitioner could reach. The conditions of native society are such as to necessitate female help for the relief of suffering and the healing of disease among the women of India.

Many other things have to be done by the agents of the Seoni mission that need not be mentioned in detail, but it would scarcely be right to omit reference to the **training of young men for the ministry** begun a few years ago by Mr McNeel. One of the students – the son of one of the first converts from heathenism – was licensed as a preacher in the month of January, and another is expected to be licensed very soon. These facts tell of much labour expended by the missionary in charge, but they also tell of fruit reaped in our mission field.

That account was published in 1904. When, twenty years later, Free Church work was restarted independently, it followed Seoni's pattern, on a smaller scale.

Expatriates and nationals have been involved in three main types of diaconal activity as the Free Church of Central India has developed. After learning a little about the people who went as missionaries, we look at the three strands – **orphanage, educational** and **health work** – before considering the church as such.

serving not only the Raj

Some extracts from "The Monthly Record" 1910 – 1920 give an idea of activities in those early days:

John McNeel reported in 1916:
The work in all its departments has suffered more or less on account of the plague, which has continued in our midst throughout the whole year. The area affected included the town of Seoni and the villages within a radius of about twenty miles. During the worst phases of the epidemic, the schools were reduced in attendance, the medical and zenana work interrupted, and many villages closed to our catechists.

*In **Chhapara**, Dulichand and Dukloo were occupied chiefly with teaching in the school but in the evenings twice a week they preached in the bazaar. In company with Mr Thomas the headmaster, they visited nearby villages on Saturdays and school holidays. At **Lakhnadon**, Daniel Cameron has preached regularly in all the villages within a radius of four miles. The total number of hearers for the year was about three thousand. On 4th March he and four other catechists visited the "Marh Mela", a fair held for four days annually seven miles north of Lakhnadon, in connection with worship of the god Shiv. Hundreds of people gathered at that place, especially from the northern parts of the district, and they heard the Word gladly.*

***Dhuma** is a new out-station in the Lakhnadon circle. It was opened in November 1915. The catechists, Puran Lall and Jian Singh, are meeting with some encouragement.*

In February I went with Thomas Curr, Aiyub, and John Laxman to the bazaar at Ugli, where we had an excellent meeting. For more than two hours the crowd stood in a solid ring around the preachers. After books were distributed the people did not disperse although darkness was coming on; so preaching continued for another half-hour. The preachers did not reach Keolari, where they were staying, fourteen miles away, until one o'clock next morning.

Dr Grant told of a village visit:
Radhabai, our faithful old Biblewoman, and I set out before noon. The road, a mere cart-track, was so uneven in places that we could only cling to the tonga and hope it wouldn't capsize. While going quickly down a sharp incline, we heard a rough grating sound and jumped out of the tonga in time to see one of its

wheels roll away and the tonga *fall with a crash to the ground. The axle had broken right across! We went back to the nearest village and the first man we spoke to turned out to be a blacksmith. After some persuasion and the promise of a rupee, he agreed to repair it and set off with our driver to view the damage. As we were known in that village, a crowd soon gathered round. One woman joined in our singing. She had lived in Seoni as a girl and had been taught by one of our* zenana *workers. She seemed quite proud of herself! Many were the demands for treatment. But as the medicine-chest was in the* tonga *a quarter of a mile away, I could please the women only by feeling the pulse of some and giving advice about their ailments.*

She told too of less exciting days at the clinic in Seoni:

Monday: *I spoke on the Second Coming of Christ, as we had talked of His Ascension on Saturday. So many of the women seem really interested. An interesting patient was a Muslim who had been ill for one and a half years. Her husband would never permit her to come but, now that she is quite unfit for work, he has arranged for her to come in a* tonga *every day. She casually mentioned that her baby, six months old, is a tea drinker. The child has been having tea every morning since she was two or three months old! Another Muslim patient came from a village ten miles away. She has had no fewer than eighteen children, of whom thirteen are dead. The last died fifteen days ago and, since then, the poor woman has been ill. Compared herself to a mango tree, which bears much fruit, little of which reaches maturity.*

Fifty-six patients altogether.

Tuesday: *One new patient was a Brahman from a village twelve miles away. Had never been in Dispensary previously and had never heard the gospel; wore a string of beads on her neck, given her by a priest at Jagannath, where she had gone on pilgrimage; twirls each bead while repeating the words, "Sita Ram". Glad that, owing to fewness of patients, had an opportunity for a private conversation with her. Another village patient is one who has left her own house and has come into town to live, as she is sure someone has cast "the evil eye" on her home. Her daughter-in-law died there, her son was ill and now her only daughter is ill. People say she has a devil, for nothing seems to do her good. I begged her to bring her daughter tomorrow, so that I may see her.*

Thirty-seven patients.

Wednesday: *One of the most tantalising and yet the most amusing was an old woman from Chownree, six miles away. The directions for applying and taking her medicines have to be told her over and over again.*

"Don't go near Miss Sahib again," our helper Bhagli says. "I've told you everything plainly."

"Yes, but ..... Bai-ji, shall I take the medicine with hot or cold water?"

I tell her as patiently as I can. She sits down on the floor, ties up a paper of ointment in one corner of her sari, a powder in another corner, then looks at her bottles. With two steps she is at my side.

"Did you say I was to **drink** the small bottle?"

I satisfy her on that point too, and she takes her departure, after salaaming with both hands clasped on her forehead.

The woman with the bewitched daughter didn't bring her, as her son has commenced some medicine which she is to take for seven days. If she is not better, he will bring her then. That makes one feel small.

Fifty-seven patients.

Thursday: Spoke on the Lord's Prayer. Not one knew the meaning of "prayer". While I was speaking upon God as our Father, a Jain woman said we Christians were faithful to God; they and others had forsaken Him. While I was speaking on the fourth petition, a woman rose excitedly and, pointing to this Jain, said that she and her caste wanted more than their daily bread. As soon as it was 8 a.m. they said, "Let us go and make money." The Jains are often the money-lenders.

Forty patients.

Friday: Asked what I had spoken on yesterday. Only one girl, who had not been present, knew. Her mother explained that, when she went home yesterday, she had told her all she remembered!

Very often the names of patients give one an idea of their parents' feelings when they arrived into the world. Today a nice Brahman girl was there – her name is Bipti ("trouble"). Names like Kachra ("rubbish"), Dulshni ("pain"), Rona ("weeping"), Panchcowrie ("five small coins") are often given to deceive the gods – to make them think the baby is not valued. The Muslim who likened herself to a poor mango tree returned today feeling, as she expressed it, "like a new woman. It's as if I'd been newly weighed in balances!" – like fresh goods in the market.

Forty-four patients.

Saturday: The parable of the Pharisee and the Publican. Enjoyed by all, especially when a gaily-coloured picture illustrating it was displayed.

Today a woman brought her baby who was suffering from bronchitis. The child has been ill for a month, and even brandy along with her usual dose of opium didn't cure her! Brandy is said to be a splendid thing for a cold.
Forty-nine patients in all.

I must confess that in 1989, when rewriting the notes for that Thursday of seventy years ago, I question the depth of my own knowledge of the meaning of prayer.

II THOSE SENT TO SERVE

'Whom shall I send . . . ?' [Isa. 6.8]
'As the Father has sent me, I am sending you.' [John 20.21]

Anchor Line's 'Cilicia' off Gibralter

4
Pioneers from Scotland

New missionaries during the period 1900-25:
**Rev. Gilbert Dick; Miss Elizabeth Macleod; Dr Annie Mackay;
Rev. Evan and Mrs Eva Mackenzie**

GILBERT DICK
An appeal for recruits for Seoni, made by the Secession Church, was reprinted in "The Monthly Record" of February 1902. Two individuals responded. Gilbert Dick of Dunblane was a young graduate who had just finished training for the ministry of the United Free Church. His offer of service was accepted. He was then ordained as a Free Church missionary to India by the Presbytery of Glasgow at Hope Street Free Church on 12th October 1905. It was hoped that he would re-establish a Free Church mission after spending one year at Seoni. Even two months before he left Scotland, however, there was a hint of difficulties ahead: "..... no accommodation for Dick in the Seoni bungalow".

Arrangements were begun to hand over the northern part of the Secession area to him. But by the next hot season he was in Calcutta, requesting his home committee that he be allowed to stay there or go to a hill station for language study, or that he be relocated to South Africa. Perhaps loneliness overwhelmed him. Perhaps Seoni's rather authoritarian ways did not suit him. At this distance we do not know. By August 1906 he was in Scotland again. "No question affecting the life and character of Mr Dick was involved....." and the Glasgow Presbytery accepted his resignation. I have not succeeded in tracing his later history.

ELIZABETH MACLEOD
The other recruit for Seoni was Elizabeth Macleod. Her father, the Rev. Ewan Macleod from Harris, was one of the twenty-six ministers who, in 1900, had decided not to enter the Union. In the Oban manse, Elizabeth and her sister Catherine grew up to be well-educated, cultured ladies, of slight physique but strong character. Elizabeth studied at Burnbank Missionary Training Home in Glasgow for two years before leaving for

51

India in November 1905. The very first issue of the Free Church young
people's magazine "The Instructor" in October 1906 carried her picture.
Subsequent issues contained many interesting accounts of her life in Seoni,
and later in Chhapara and Lakhnadon.

As a Biblewoman, Elizabeth spent much time in *zenana* quarters of
Indian homes. (The word *"zenana"*, dropped from missionary parlance
about mid-century, is still used in colloquial speech. Rail coaches have
zenana compartments, reserved for women and children.) Elizabeth and
other Biblewomen taught Hindu and Muslim women to read (and what
better text-book than the Bible?); to write at least their own names; sewing,
knitting, child care and basic health matters. By the time she retired (for
the first time!) in 1944, women in Indian society were no longer kept in
such strict seclusion. Although *zenana* work as such has been discontinued,
there is still a preference in Asian culture today for the mixing of men and
women to be less free than is usual in Western society. When Free Church
ladies now give time to teaching English as a second language to home-
makers of other cultures in Scottish cities, they, like Elizabeth in those
days, hope to demonstrate God's love in action.

Having spent twenty years in Seoni, Elizabeth Macleod tended to follow
the well-tried ways of the Rev. John McNeel. He, although an American,
believed that traditional (British!) methods were best. The Rev. Murray
MacLeod, a young minister of different outlook, arrived from Scotland in
1933. He was eager to conform to Indian cultural patterns as far as they
were compatible with Christian values. Elizabeth was not hide-bound. She
assessed the situation wisely and, recognising that the newcomer's heart
was in the right place, she gave him every encouragement. After she died
on 24th May 1959, the Rev. Professor R. A. Finlayson, who was a shrewd
judge of character, wrote a tribute to her. He drew attention to her
"gentleness and firmness, modesty and sagacity". Indian people, sensitive
to genuine spirituality, spoke of her with the utmost respect.

ANNIE MACKAY

Annie Mackay, born in Canada, was twelve years old when the family
settled in Scotland. Her mother died a few years later in the Kingussie
manse. "Some of you may become missionaries ....." she said to the children
gathered round.

At that time ladies were not admitted to classes at Edinburgh University's
Medical School, although they were allowed to sit exams there. They
studied at Surgeons' Hall. She was often a visitor with other young people
to the manse of Fountainbridge Free Church (later St Columba's). The
minister there, the Rev. Alexander Stewart, had, with the congregation,
entered the Free Church from the Free Presbyterian in 1905. He and one

of his elders, Walter R. T. Sinclair, exercised a powerful influence on behalf of foreign missions. The Foreign Missions' Committee gave Annie Mackay a small bursary and at the end of her studies asked her where she would like to serve. She said she would prefer Peru, where her brother the Rev. Calvin Mackay had gone in 1917, but was willing to go anywhere.

To Seoni she went in 1921, arriving during an epidemic of plague – a rat-borne disease that had been ravaging India for a quarter of a century since it had come in from China. Like Elizabeth Macleod before her, Annie Mackay studied Urdu with a local teacher. When they went north to Chhapara and Lakhnadon in 1925, they were among people whose mother-tongue was Hindi. Hindi was these missionaries' third language. Later recruits had the great advantage of Hindi study at the Missionary Language School at Landour, six thousand feet above sea level in the Himalayan foothills.

From 1901, the Free Church had contributed to the foreign missions' funds of the Secession Church. With two missionaries of her own in India from 1921, it was time to try again to start a separate Free Church of Scotland work. As had been agreed in 1905, the Secession would hand over responsibility for the northern half of its area, that is, the Lakhnadon *Tehsil* – the one thousand six hundred square miles over which the Law Court in Lakhnadon has jurisdiction. During 1923, "The Monthly Record" repeatedly carried an appeal for an ordained missionary, preferably a married man, to superintend the work. A copy of the magazine was lent by Dr Jeannie Grant of Seoni, who was on holiday in Kalimpong, to the Rev. Evan Mackenzie, a Church of Scotland missionary there. He noticed the appeal and responded to it. He was accepted into the Free Church and, in April 1924, he and his wife Eva (née Anderson) arrived at Lakhnadon.

EVAN AND EVA MACKENZIE

Evan Mackenzie was born in 1868 and grew up at Dores on the shores of Loch Ness. He became a member of the Free North Church, Inverness. In 1894 he and his first wife, Elizabeth (née Macrae), joined the Tibetan Pioneer Mission. Tibet was a closed land then as now. Two years later they transferred from that Mission to the work at Kalimpong, not far from Tibet. In 1909, the local Presbytery in the Church of Scotland Mission there licensed and ordained him. He wrote "A Life of Christ" in Tibetan, and translated "The Pilgrim's Progress". His wife Elizabeth died in 1917 and he later remarried. Dr Grant wrote of him: "as ready with a pick and shovel as with a pen". Professor John R. Mackay of the Free Church College, who had heard Evan Mackenzie lecture on Tibet, commented on his "manly presence, intelligent look and power of giving an understandable account (of Tibet)".

In 1924, John McNeel had arranged for the Free Church to buy a fifteen-acre field on the outskirts of Lakhnadon village, the field where the hospital is today. However, Evan Mackenzie preferred high ground, as healthier and giving prominence to the Christian presence. A hill site of five acres, the *Toriya* ("the little hill"), less than a mile from Lakhnadon, was gifted and construction work began. He hoped to build there a large complex of housing – for missionaries, Indian workers, orphans and servants – and a church that would be obvious to all around. There was some misunderstanding between McNeel and Mackenzie, both good men. McNeel knew the local situation well, while Mackenzie had wide experience of church work in the mountains. When ill-health forced Evan Mackenzie to resign three years later, in 1927, the building programme on the *Toriya* was less than half complete. In 1930, having recovered somewhat from serious kidney disease, Evan Mackenzie was inducted to the Glenmoriston congregation of the Church of Scotland. He died in 1934.

Elizabeth Macleod returned to Seoni in November 1925 after her third home leave. She and Annie Mackay were eager to move as soon as possible to the new Free Church area. At that time the Mackenzies were ill in a Calcutta hospital. On 10th December 1925, Miss Elizabeth and Dr Annie (as they were affectionately known) came the twenty-one miles north from Seoni to Chhapara in Mr McNeel's car, their luggage going on ahead by bullock cart. They rented an upstairs room in the home of a respected Muslim land-owner and were given permission for medical work to be done on the ground-floor verandah.

A small house in its own grounds nearer the main road had been used by workers of the Seoni Mission. John McNeel kindly saw to its renovation for the ladies, and did the work thoroughly. After sixty years' occupancy by missionaries, the walls of that home could tell many stories today!

For two decades Miss Elizabeth and Dr Annie were missionaries together, working in Chhapara and Lakhnadon. Each taking after her father, they were evangelists at heart. Institutional work in school, orphanage and dispensaries was cared for, but never to the neglect of spiritual priorities. Dr Annie continued in India until 1966, retiring after forty-four years in harness. Her legacy of goodwill there lasts even now. She retired to Inverness, sharing a flat with her sister Catherine. You might meet them there today, in 1989, walking by the River Ness.

Elizabeth Macleod   *Annie M. Mackay*

Evan Mackenzie

seeking to understand

During the world-wide epidemic of influenza in 1918, Elizabeth Macleod wrote from Seoni:

Practically all mission work except the medical is at a standstill at present, because of the influenza-pneumonia epidemic. Dr Grant has come back from Scotland just in time for very hard work and there is far more to do than she can undertake..... Since beginning this letter, I have been to Chhindwara, forty miles from here, to see a Swedish missionary, an old friend of Bible Training Home days in Glasgow. She was ill with influenza. Now I have heard of her death. She was one of the most devoted of workers and seemed so much needed just where she was. It is one of the mysteries which we cannot understand now.

What she did understand of God's grace she was concerned to tell. Writing of a day at a busy bazaar:

What multitudes of men and women! There were literally hundreds of Gondh women. As they all gazed at us in fear, or wonder, or with kind and friendly interest, it was with a feeling of shame that we looked back into their faces. Do we not owe them something we have been withholding? Is the gospel ours, to keep it to ourselves? I daresay the feelings of most in that crowded bazaar might be summed up in the words of one who, when asked about worshipping stones, replied, "What can we do? That is all we know." It is good to bring the "good news". But sometimes, sitting among the women in these villages, one does not know what to say to them, nor how to say it so that they may understand.

Of another occasion Elizabeth wrote:

We walked across the fields, as there is no tonga road. One man lifted a stick high above his head and said, "Suppose this is a very high tree. You cannot climb up into it. But if you put stones at the foot of the tree, then you can climb up. So God is high above us, but these idols enable us to reach Him."

And again:

We sang and spoke to the women at the government dispensary in Lakhnadon. One was a widow. Although of a well-to-do family she wore poor clothing, no jewellery, and ate only once a day. Tea served in enamel bowls (from the Dispensary?) was brought for us. When we had drunk it, we were asked to put the bowls on the ground, and a dog was called to sup up what was left at the bottom. After we had gone, the sweeper would remove these dishes. This was a Brahman family and no-one would touch the dishes after we had used them.

Elizabeth would not have recognised the word **contextualisation**, such a favourite today with missiologists. But she, of all our missionaries in India, seems to have agonised most over how to make the eternal Word plain to people whose thought patterns were so different from her own.

5

Scots plus Irish

New missionaries during the period 1925-50:
**Dr Willie and Mrs Marion Urquhart; Miss Lena Gillies;
Rev. Murray and Mrs Sarah MacLeod; Miss Edith Stewart;
Miss Anna Stewart; Miss Nan Dunlop; Miss Darla Mackenzie;
Miss Janette Brown; Rev. George and Mrs Babs Sutherland**

Those who continued:
**Miss Elizabeth Macleod; Dr Annie Mackay;
Rev. Evan and Mrs Eva Mackenzie**

WILLIE AND MARION URQUHART
In 1926, Dr Willie Urquhart came to
Lakhnadon. Rev. Evan Mackenzie was
overjoyed to welcome his "Joshua", as
he called him. Born in Kyle of Lochalsh
in 1904, Willie as a boy had played
barefoot on the rocky hillside there with
Malcolm Macrae, later a missionary in
Cajamarca, Peru. During the 1920s,
hundreds of post-war students crowded
Scotland's Universities. Many were
enthused for Christian mission by Dr
John A. Mackay, who was on home-leave
in Scotland after pioneering Free Church
work in Lima, Peru. One such was
Kenneth Mackay of Alness Schoolhouse
and later of Moyobamba, Peru. He
graduated in Medicine in Glasgow at the
same time as Willie Urquhart in
Edinburgh. In his old age, Dr Kenneth,
with a twinkle in his eye, told how they
had played truant together from some

*Willie Urquhart with a
tracheotomy patient and
dispenser.*

classes during their one session at the Free Church College. In spite of that they were ordained for missionary service!

Before settling into the work at Lakhnadon, Dr Urquhart went to Landour Language School. Visiting the McNeels' daughters from Seoni at an American boarding school there, he heard familiar Scottish songs being sung. A year later the singer, Marion Wright, a governess from Dumfriesshire, became his wife. The Little Bungalow on the *Toriya* was habitable, while work continued on the main part of the Big Bungalow. (The wings planned earlier were never built.) Willie Urquhart's building expertise was nil. There was no contractor, materials were scarce, workmen lethargic, climate and disease a burden. In 1930, after four years in India, he returned to Scotland with his family. But in a culture which values such things, he was remembered at Lakhnadon as one who kept his temper! Thirty years later, in General Practice at Bishopbriggs, Glasgow, he loved to tell how he used to walk over the hill-top site early each morning, praying that it would be like a beacon of light to surrounding villages. He died in 1964.

LENA GILLIES

Some months after the Urquharts were invalided home, a Biblewoman, Dolina Gillies (or Lena, as she likes to be called) went to India. During her childhood in Staffin on the Isle of Skye, she had read biographies of David Livingstone and Mary Slessor. At home and at church – the United Free Church – she was encouraged to prepare for missionary service. During her three years at the Bible Training Institute in Glasgow, she became a member of Govan Free Church. She then took a brief course in Tropical Health in London. Her first term of service was of five years' duration, but her second lasted from 1936 until 1944 as the war interfered with travel. However, when her mother died in 1944, she came home to care for the family.

Later, she married James Brown from Edinburgh and they settled in Skye. Two of Lena's cousins are Free Church ministers in Glasgow at the time of writing – the Rev. John A. Gillies in Partick Highland, and the Rev. Donald N. Macleod in Grant Street. Grown-up orphans in Chhapara, especially the Rev. Prakash Kumar, remember Lena with affection. The most treasured possession of Charan Masih, who was cook to Chhapara missionaries for many years, was Lena's gift to him of her big Hindi Bible.

MURRAY AND SARAH MACLEOD

Malcolm Murray Macleod, born of Lewis parents in Dunoon, was influenced at the Free Church College by Miss Elizabeth Macleod's address to the students' Missionary Society there. He married Sarah Morrison, who was known affectionately as "Gipsy" and was a trained nurse. They went to Lakhnadon in 1933. Soon, Murray Macleod had an excellent grasp of Hindi and was highly thought of by Indian and Scottish colleagues. Learning about Hinduism, he became disturbed by similarities between infant baptism and a Hindu rite which confirmed tiny children in their caste. He corresponded with several prominent Free Church men about this and continued his study during home-leave. When, in the early forties, he became convinced that infant baptism was not biblical, he offered to resign. Wartime conditions made replacement difficult. At the request of the Foreign Missions' Committee he continued in the ministry at Lakhnadon and Chhapara, neither pressing his Baptist views on others nor baptising infants.

In 1949, he left to be pastor of Union Church in Ootacamund, a South Indian hill resort. After three years, he moved to a Baptist church in Glasgow, and from there to Canada. For twelve years he lectured in New Testament Exegesis and Missions at Toronto Bible College. The Macleods are now retired in Ontario.

EDITH STEWART

The Rev. Dr Alexander Stewart of St Columba's Free Church, Edinburgh, was a force for missions in his own home as well as in the church. Two of his five children became missionaries at Lakhnadon and Chhapara. Mr Graham Anderson, a cousin of his wife, stayed at the manse in 1930 during home-leave from service with the China Inland Mission. Under his influence the youngest daughter, Edith, determined to be a missionary. She left Art College in favour of the University on her father's advice. After graduating M.A. she studied for a year at the Bible Training Institute in Glasgow; then had a little nursing experience at Chalmers Hospital in Edinburgh.

Her own inclination was strongly towards China, or to Dohnavur in South India. Amy Carmichael, founder of the Dohnavur Fellowship, was a practical idealist whose books urge whole-hearted commitment to Christ. No doubt her father's concern as Convener of the Free Church Foreign Missions' Committee helped keep Edith within her own church. Even so, he was heart-broken to see her leave home for India. Edith went to Lakhnadon in 1935. Her mother died the following year, and Dr Stewart himself in 1937.

ANNA STEWART

Edith's older sister, Anna, was an English teacher at Penicuik School. After their mother died, she felt more free to join Edith. In March 1937, she told her father that God was calling her to work in India. It was a shock to him, but he said he would not stand in her way. He urged her to

Edith Stewart's marriage (1938)
Back row l. to r. Sarah Macleod, M. Murray Macleod and son,
Lena Gillies, Annie Mackay.
Front row l. to r. Anna Stewart, Jack Dain and Edith, Elizabeth Macleod.

apply at once to the Committee. Financial stringency made the Committee hesitate. The Rev. George Mackay of Fearn pled that she be sent as a memorial to her father, who had died suddenly following emergency surgery. Ultimately, in September 1938, the Women's Foreign Missionary Association paid her fare, and she arrived in India in time to be Edith's bridesmaid. Although their service as single ladies was short, the Stewart sisters brought new life and encouragement to the Christians in Chhapara and Lakhnadon.

Within three years, Anna too had married. The fortunate bridegrooms had been their fellow-students at Language School. Edith married Jack Dain, a missionary with the Regions Beyond Missionary Union in Bihar. Soon after the outbreak of war in 1939, he was called up and served in the Indian Navy as an officer. Returning to Britain in 1946, he became Home Secretary of the Zenana Bible and Medical Mission (later the Bible and Medical Missionary Fellowship, and now Interserve International). In 1959, he was ordained and moved to Sydney as Federal Secretary of the Australian Church Missionary Society. After six years there, he was appointed a Bishop under Archbishop Marcus Loane. He and Edith had many good years there. She died in 1985, her Christian testimony bright throughout her fight with cancer.

In 1941, at Lakhnadon, Anna Stewart married the Rev. Cyril Thomson, a missionary with the Bible Churchmen's Missionary Society (B.C.M.S.), an evangelical Anglican body. To enable Anna to remain in the Free Church Mission, Cyril was prepared to leave B.C.M.S. and join the Free Church. He visited Lakhnadon several times and was happy to work with Murray Macleod. However, the Foreign Missions' Committee asked him to attend a course at the Free Church College in Edinburgh. This he was unwilling to do, having had four years' training at the B.C.M.S. College in Bristol and a two-year curacy in England. During this impasse, Cyril joined the Indian Army, as did many other missionaries. At the time of his marriage to Anna, he was a staff officer. They remained in India until 1948, their last two years being in Calcutta, where Cyril helped to found Indian Youth for Christ. He was used in the conversion of many young people, including David John, now Free Church minister in Jabalpur. One of the Thomsons' children, Robin, has given over twenty years' service in India in the field of theological education, mainly at Union Bible Seminary, Pune, Maharashtra.

NAN DUNLOP

If the Stewart sisters' time with the Free Church in India was short, the next recruit spent ten times as long there. Annie J. Dunlop, better known as Nan, gave thirty-one years of faithful service. From her earliest years, her mother had encouraged her to be a missionary. After a hazardous wartime voyage, she arrived in India in 1944. At Lakhnadon and Chhapara she helped to update medical facilities. Like Janette Brown a few years later, Nan was seconded to the Church of Scotland's Mure Memorial Hospital in Nagpur for some months when their Nursing School was desperately short of tutors. In that connection she was a member of the Mid-India Board of Examiners.

Capable nurse and midwife though she is, it is as a teller of "the old, old story" and as mother to our orphan children that she is best remembered. She is in her element on village visits. Describing events in the life of Christ and their significance, Nan uses local dialect and dramatic gestures to great effect. She pours out her love on people, and they know it. Although retired, Nan still visits India as often as possible. When she resigned because of ill-health in 1975, the Chairman of the Foreign Missions' Board commented on "her rare mixture of grace and grit".

DARLA MACKENZIE

"She has done what she could," said a colleague about Darla (Catherine) Mackenzie's brief service. Born and brought up at Lochluichart, in Ross-shire, where her father was head gardener, she cared for her parents as they became elderly. She was accepted as a Biblewoman when already middle-aged, and spent most of 1946 in India. Language study was hard for her. Adjustment to village culture with poverty and disease at very close quarters proved difficult. She resumed her duties as postmistress at Muir-of-Ord, and for thirty-three more years, until her death, she encouraged many in mission work at home and overseas, both church-based and interdenominational. Her time in India had not been wasted.

JANETTE BROWN

Janette Brown's father was Walter Rounsfell Brown, a Glasgow lawyer and the Free Church's first Foreign Missions' Convener after 1900. The family worshipped at Milton Free Church, a missionary-minded congregation. Mr Brown did not agree with Janette's suggestion that she apply to the Free Church College in preparation for missionary service. At her interview with the Committee she asked about attending a Missionary Training College. Like other lay applicants over the years she was assured that a Free Church background was all she needed!

With an Arts degree and eight years' experience as a Health Visitor, Janette arrived in India a few months before Independence Day. The gaining of independence on 15th August 1947 coincided with Partition. On her way back from Landour Language School to Chhapara, Janette was caught up in the resulting intercommunal riots. Delayed at Dehra Dun Railway Station for two weeks, she helped in emergency treatment of casualties.

The work that followed at Chhapara was more routine – village visits with Indian Biblewomen; maternity work in homes; attending to patients at the Dispensary; winter camps; overseeing the Chhapara Mission School; teaching there and in Sunday School; and administrative duties, especially accounts. Trying to make ends meet at the School with a small grant from Scotland and an uncertain one from the Indian Government was a constant headache. Nearest to her heart was the all-round care of the orphan children, a responsibility she shared with foster-mother Gajaribai. There were some disagreements, as when Gajaribai frowned on the introduction of carrots to the children's menu, or when a senior missionary warned that even a weekly egg for each child would be far too expensive. Janette was delighted with a huge mosquito-net sent from home in 1948. It was large enough to cover a child's cot as well as her own bed!

While on home-leave in 1952, she studied at Moray House, gaining her Diplomas in Education and in Religious Education. These were useful both then and later, for, after returning to Scotland in 1957, she took up teaching there. Some years later she married Andrew Gailey, manager of a coal mine. In childhood, Janette and her brother Walter had been given a stamp collection – that of Archibald McNeilage, a Free Church worthy and friend of their father. This interest in stamps was rekindled at Landour Language School when she met people of many nationalities. Back in Edinburgh, Janette became a licensed stamp dealer in 1967. Her activities in that direction have raised thousands of pounds for missions. She is still an active member of Buccleuch and Greyfriars Free Church in Edinburgh.

GEORGE AND BABS SUTHERLAND

As Murray Macleod had been challenged by Elizabeth Macleod when she appealed in 1932 for an ordained man for India, so George Sutherland was challenged by Annie Mackay in 1948. George belonged to a Church of Scotland family in Dornie, Wester Ross. He was employed before the war both as an electrician at Kinlochleven, and in forestry. After service in the Royal Air Force, he studied at Edinburgh University and the Free Church College. His wife Margot Davidson, known as Babs, was of Baptist background, and trained as a graduate teacher. The Sutherlands, with their two children, went to Lakhnadon in 1950. The *Toriya* again heard happy sounds of little ones! During the ups and downs of life, Babs was a tower of strength.

The mission buildings at that time were in urgent need of repair. During the winter months of 1954-55, the Convener of the Foreign Missions' Committee, the Rev. Duncan Leitch, and his wife visited India. One of his recommendations was that more living accommodation for medical and nursing staff be provided at the hospital. George's artisan skills were invaluable. Some might be offended by the tribute, but, to health-conscious people, installation of Lakhnadon's first-ever septic tanks was a great feat. He was in full sympathy with hard-pressed medical staff and often drove them out himself to distant villages on emergency calls. He worked strenuously to obtain medical goods at a time when the Government's suspicion of Christian missionaries hindered supply.

One of his last duties at Lakhnadon was on 7th October 1959. On that day, with permission from Edinburgh and with assistance from colleagues in Seoni, he conducted the ordination and induction service of the Rev. Prakash Kumar, the first-fruits, so to speak, of the missionaries' efforts to establish a local church. After resigning in 1959, George spent three more years in the Free Church ministry, at Minard, Argyll. In 1963, he went to Rajasthan (West India) as a Church of Scotland missionary and served there for twelve years. At his funeral service at St Andrews in March 1988, he was remembered with affection and appreciation, and special mention was made of his building skills in the villages of Rajasthan. Babs died fourteen months later.

Nan Dunlop cuts the ribbon at the extension of Lakhnadon Hospital, 6 April 1982.

Darla MacKenzie with a grand nephew.

Janette Brown

George and Babs Sutherland (right) with their children: also Mary MacDonald (left) and Annie MacKay (centre).

from morning to night

In 1930, soon after Lena Gillies went from the Isle of Skye to Chhapara, Elizabeth Macleod wrote home, "She has come to us like a breath from the Highland hills. Now she is working hard at Hindi."

Lena (now Mrs Brown) has helped me reconstruct the outline of a typical day at Chhapara, in April 1933.

4 a.m: During the hot summer season, most people sleep outside. Daylight comes early, but not before the women in homes across the lane behind the bungalow begin to grind wheat for their families' daily bread. The grinding stones sound a soft grrr..... grrr..... grrr.....

5 a.m: Since about 1 a.m. it has been almost cool. Now bullock carts rumble up the rough road and dust thickens the air. Before long, the sun's rays will be fierce again.

6 a.m: Breakfast on the front verandah, which faces south towards the school. This meal is called chhoti hazari *– literally "small presence": an odd name! Charan, the cook, brings Miss Elizabeth and Lena a tray each, with a tiny boiled egg, diminutive pieces of toast, home-made marmalade, buffalo butter and tea.*

Although the bungalow is very close to Chhapara's main street, not far from where it joins the Nagpur-Jabalpur road, the verandah gives good privacy. It is deep, and shaded by bougainvillaea.

7 a.m: Family worship on the verandah with the orphan children, Shanta (who cares for them) and Charan. They sing a section of Psalm 119 in Hindi to the tune "Kilmarnock". Then each person who can read takes a verse in turn of today's Scripture passage – part of 2 Samuel chapter 15 – about David's escape from Absalom and the loyalty of Ittai the Gittite. David's words to Ittai, "May mercy and truth be with you," are echoed in prayer, simple and reverent. "Mercy and truth" – how like a bullock cart's two wheels, each complementing the other, thinks Lena.

After worship, Shanta tells what she will need to buy today for the children's food, and Lena gives her money. Mental note: for the **"Orphans"** *account.*

8 a.m: Miss Elizabeth sets off for Seoni to see about next session's grant for the school. It will be a wearisome day. She travels twenty-one miles each way by bus, and hires a horse-tonga in Seoni for her visits to government offices.

Dr Annie comes from Lakhnadon on Tuesdays and Saturdays only, so she won't be in Chhapara today. Compounder-Biblewoman Rahilbai has already collected the Dispensary keys from the bungalow. She supervises cleaning and sets out medicines. Tablets come by rail to Seoni (from the Mission Tablet Industry factory, a Methodist concern, in South India) but she makes up mixtures herself.

Lena follows Rahilbai to the Dispensary, taking a short-cut by back lanes. There's great activity at the well, women and girls chattering as they draw water and wash clothes. They call a cheery greeting. The potter is busy making huge water-pots today. Bantam hens scratch in the dust round Muslim homes. That must be a sick cow tethered at the pundit's — all the others were taken out to graze at daybreak.

The narrow lane leading to the Dispensary's side-entrance is dirty — very dirty. Flies buzz up in swarms. And the stench!

Rahil makes sure the Dispensary compound is kept clean. She has the books ready for staff prayers. Neither of the two Hindu women-helpers can read. One listens intently. She is of a caste from whose hand any Hindu, even a Brahman, will drink, which simplifies life for the patients.

Not very many patients have come today. Unlike Lena, Rahil understands the country dialect and knows each of the "regulars" well. Some make an excuse of any small complaint to escape from mother-in-law's domain for an hour or two! They love listening to gospel lyrics. And Lena loves telling them of the Saviour.

9 a.m: Rahil has managed to remove a grain-seed from a child's ear. Everyone congratulates her on her skill with the big syringe. Since she is coping so well, Lena leaves her and spends over an hour in a Jain home, close by the Jain temple. The two teenage girls there, one the daughter and the other a daughter-in-law of the cloth-merchant, are learning to read and write Hindi. The grandparents will not allow them to attend school. Before coming away, Lena reads with them a passage from the Bible and explains its meaning. At this stage, the older women too gather around. Their favourite passage is at the end of chapter 8 of Luke's gospel.

*11 a.m: Back now to the Mission School in time to teach a Scripture lesson. Discipline is good. There are fifty-eight 12-13 year-olds, mostly boys, in today's class. They study the eighth commandment. Do teachers realise how influential their **attitudes** are, as well as their words, wonders Lena, as she strives to explain God's standards.*

12:30 p.m: Miss Elizabeth is not back from Seoni, so Lena is alone at lunch. As usual, Charan has prepared their favourite wheat porridge served with buffalo milk, which is scarce in this weather. Then there is rice and lentils (no vegetables today – they too are rare in summer) and a big pot of tea.

After the fierce heat outside, Lena appreciates the current of air from the big fan overhead, but feels sorry for the old widow who works the clumsy contraption.

She, on the other hand, is grateful for any work because of the pay it brings. Before lying down for a brief rest, Lena sprinkles water around her bedroom to cool it down.

2 p.m: Rahil and Lena go out to visit women in the zenana *quarters of their homes. Lena wears the foreigners' customary* topi *(sun helmet), while Rahil draws her sari over her head. Others think them foolish to go out in the heat of the day. But this is a comparatively peaceful time of day for the women they visit. Their husbands are at work, or asleep – depending mainly on whether they are poor or rich.*

Small children play on the floor. Miss Elizabeth and Rahil have been visiting many of the women for years, so some of what they hear today is not new to them. One young woman in the silversmiths' joint family is eager to practise her English. She went to school in Bombay before her parents moved to Chhapara. She came from her in-laws ten days ago to await the birth of her first child. Another girl in that home shows her beautiful needlework. They insist that the visitors taste a choice mango from their garden. How different this well-to-do household is from many poor homes that the ladies visit! Rich or poor, all are very friendly.

5 p.m: Rahil must return to her chores now and cook the evening meal. Lena sits out on the verandah where the children soon find her. Their energy is amazing, even in summer's scorching heat! One nestles her head in Lena's lap and tells all about the quarrel with her best friend at school today.

Once the sun is low in the west, they walk to the bridge where a breeze wafts up from the river. It is almost dark when they return. The children scamper home to see what Shanta has for their evening meal.

7 p.m: About 6 o'clock, Miss Elizabeth came back from Seoni. Over dinner she tells of her day – frustrating delays in government offices, but a promise of the grant to be paid by July. She enjoyed meeting old friends, and had lunch at the Mission Bungalow.

Charan serves pumpkin in cheese sauce, and potatoes. The cheese is a luxury, a gift from Swedish Lutheran friends at Chhindwara, west of Seoni. Meat is not available in Chhapara and Charan is rarely able to get fish. When he does, he makes sure he buys it alive! Tonight he serves a hot-weather treat – delicious mango fool.

8 p.m: Lena's last duty is to take evening worship with the orphan children and Shanta, in their own wee home. Then they spread bedding in the courtyard and are soon asleep.

The runner bringing mail daily from Seoni had nothing for the mission bungalow today. Mail could be sent by bus, but perhaps the Post Office authorities are kind to the relays of runners, men who value this employment. By lamplight Lena attends to accounts but is too tired to concentrate. Mosquitoes and other insects are troublesome. In spite of the noise of wedding celebrations nearby, Miss Elizabeth and Lena, safely under their mosquito nets, are soon relaxing in bed, in the cooler air outside.

6

Australians too

New missionaries during the period 1950-70:
**Miss Mary Ann MacDonald; Dr Helen Ramsay;
Mr Mervyn and Mrs Pat Oliver; Miss Flora Macleod;
Dr Anne Urquhart; Miss Heather Beaton;
Rev. Ian and Mrs Alina McKenzie**

Those who continued:
**Dr Annie Mackay; Miss Nan Dunlop;
Miss Janette Brown; Rev. George and Mrs Babs Sutherland**

MARY ANN MACDONALD
After Elizabeth Macleod retired Dr Annie Mackay found a second boon companion in Mary Ann MacDonald, a true "salt of the earth" person from Bernera, Lewis. With experience as a district nurse, she served in India from 1951 to 1971, with a gap of four years in the sixties to care for her parents. She returned to India in 1979 for seven months to be with the teenage orphan boys in Jabalpur. Overhearing some criticism of a man of God, Mary quickly quoted Psalm 105 verse 15, "Touch not mine anointed, and do my prophets no harm." She reinforced her quotation at the earliest opportunity by giving a big kiss to the one criticised. This attitude was infectious. The report of the Foreign Missions' Board's delegates after their visit to India in 1972 noted the harmony existing among missionaries, in spite of marked differences of opinion.

We did not grudge her to her elderly parents; nor to Maxwell House Eventide Home when she became matron there in 1974. But India felt much the poorer for her going. How right was the wise woman who, shortly before Mary was born, advised the mother-to-be that this child would be a servant of the Lord! Three weeks before she went to glory I was privileged to bring her up-to-date news and pictures of many who still love her in India. That meeting with Mary Ann at 17 Morrison Avenue, Stornoway, on 24th August 1988 is a precious memory. She was, as usual, relishing a cup of scalding hot, black tea. Her sense of humour undimmed, the winsome smile and light in her eyes spoke volumes of her love for people; and all because she knew her Lord's great love for her.

HELEN RAMSAY
Dr Helen Ramsay's service spanned thirty years: 1955-85. Her father, the Rev. Malcolm Ramsay, minister of the Manning River congregation in the Presbyterian Church of Eastern Australia, had trained at the Free Church College in Edinburgh and had married Helen McGregor who came of a farming family at Cawdor, near Inverness. Between graduating in Sydney and going to India, Helen spent over a year in Scotland and has revisited it several times since then. Motivated by a sense of indebtedness to Christ, she has been deeply committed to the work, in Chhapara particularly. Although under the Free Church of Scotland Foreign Missions' Board, she was supported actively by her home denomination in Australia. This brought the benefit of that church's quick responsiveness to special needs. For example, they supplied money for a car (with replacement after three years) and for improvements to Chhapara Dispensary. Not that Scotland refused such things. But the filtering of requests through the committee in Edinburgh seemed to take longer. Perhaps special appeals were allowed more readily in Australia.

Dr Ramsay initiated the plans to improve facilities at Lakhnadon Hospital, plans which were financed from Scotland and implemented in 1966. After studying at Vellore Christian Medical College's Eye Department in South India for ten weeks in 1962, she began doing cataract operations. Then Eye Camps became a regular feature of the winter months in Chhapara or Lakhnadon. She cared for her parents in Australia from 1970 to 1976 and, on her return to Chhapara, gave a strong thrust to the development of Community Health work. Her faithful second-in-command, Sister Taramoni Lall (wife of evangelist Mr Panna Lall) now runs the Chhapara Christian Health Centre, a model of efficient caring in the name of Christ. Dr Ramsay, at present working part-time in General Practice in Taree, New South Wales, is an adviser to the Missions' Committee of the Presbyterian Church of Eastern Australia.

MERVYN AND PAT OLIVER
Recommended by the Rev. W. J. Grier of the Evangelical Presbyterian Church of Ireland, Mervyn Oliver went to Lakhnadon in 1960 with experience in Christian literature work. He was energetic in going to outlying village bazaars with books and gramophone – and a loudspeaker donated by children in Lewis. Gospel Recordings make Hindi and other language records available at low cost for use in evangelism. Mervyn found his lack of ordination frustrating.

In 1963, he married Pat Hearn, daughter of a British businessman in India. Later that year, he resigned and joined the Swedish Lutheran Mission elsewhere in Madhya Pradesh. The family suffered ill-health during several years there. They have now settled in the south of England, where Mervyn is in business.

FLORA MACLEOD

With Pat Hearn and her mother on the Anchor Line boat going from Liverpool to Bombay in 1962 were two Free Church recruits: Flora Macleod and Anne Urquhart. Youngest daughter in a missionary-minded family, Flora was influenced in childhood by Elizabeth Macleod, who was on furlough from India, and by the Rev. G. N. M. Collins, minister of her home congregation – St Columba's, Edinburgh. Flora's maternal grandfather, Donald Maclean, was Professor of Church History at the Free Church College. As the first child born in a Free Church manse after the troubles of 1900, Flora's mother became known as "Una", famous later in the Free Church as "Mrs Una", secretary of the Women's Foreign Missionary Association from 1936 until 1973. Flora's father, the Rev. John Macleod O.B.E., was Foreign Missions' Convener from 1937 until his death two years later. Her brother, the Rev. D. K. Macleod, is at present Chairman of the Foreign Missions' Board.

During thirteen years of nursing service in India – from 1962 to 1975 – Flora Macleod's favourite duties were helping Nan Dunlop in the care of orphan toddlers; running a weekly clinic at Anjania village, six miles east of Chhapara; delivering babies at Lakhnadon Hospital; and assisting in theatre there. On her first home-leave, she lost no time in telling people about the sub-standard housing of the Orphanage. There was a prompt response to the W.F.M.A. appeal. The improved Orphanage building was easily adapted later for hospital purposes, forming the nucleus of the Chhapara Christian Health Centre. Flora resigned because of recurrent illness. After a deputation tour in Australia, she married (in 1976) Alex Neil, a member of the administrative staff at the University of Sydney and an elder in the Presbyterian Church of Eastern Australia. Barbara Humphries from Australia, giving one year's nursing and secretarial help at Lakhnadon in 1971, had encouraged Flora's interest in Australia.

ANNE URQUHART

Dr Anne Urquhart of Killearnan was grateful to her aunt, Dr Annie Mackay, for continuing in the work so that she could have time to study Hindi. Dr Annie was in her seventieth year when Flora and Anne arrived in 1962. During Anne's first term, facilities at Lakhnadon Hospital were improved. Members of the Foreign Missions' Board, exasperated at the women missionaries' vagueness about costs, were relieved when a businessman, the British Consul's local representative, came to the rescue. He had been most helpful when Flora Macleod had needed emergency repatriation because of serious illness in 1963. He and his colleagues provided an architect, a contractor and some skilled workmen for building extensions in 1966.

During Dr Ramsay's absence in Australia in 1972, Dr Urquhart bought a motor-cycle for easier travel between Lakhnadon and Chhapara. The next year, travelling on it from Nagpur through Kipling country near Seoni, she had an accident which resulted in a broken leg. By the time she returned from prolonged sick leave, the medical work was incorporated into the Emmanuel Hospital Association. She agreed to be seconded to E.H.A. In 1975, when needs in other hospitals were more pressing than in our own, she moved to Satbarwa in south-west Bihar. The following year, with permission from the Foreign Missions' Board, she responded to an appeal for a doctor to go to Kachhwa, U.P. The doctor recently retired from Kachhwa Hospital, Dr Nevile Everard, had filled in at Lakhnadon for a good part of Anne's sick-leave. He had even stayed on in 1973 to initiate a new recruit, Dr Donald MacDonald. After eight years at Kachhwa, she came on home-leave in 1984 and decided to stay in Scotland because of family ties. In 1989 she is working on this history project. Her application for a visa to return to medical work in India has been refused by the government in Delhi.

HEATHER BEATON

Heather Beaton comes from Newcastle in Australia, but is of Skye extraction. Before going to India in 1963, she had been in charge of a private hospital where much surgery was done. These responsibilities had prepared her well for the very different world of an Indian village hospital. Her enthusiasm for good work, her cheerfulness and her deep loyalty to patients and colleagues for Christ's sake were infectious. This ensured high standards in conditions that would have discouraged lesser souls. Nor were her gifts used only in the hospital. In next to no time she could have a tasty meal ready for any number of visitors. Her plants were so beautiful that even the District Magistrate once helped himself to several large flower-pots of ferns – with scarcely so much as a "by your leave"! In later years, Mrs Joan MacDonald was famous there too for good food and an attractive garden. In 1976, Heather went home to care for her parents. Although she returned to India in 1982, government restrictions did not allow her to stay beyond 1985. Dr Ramsay appreciated her company in Chhapara during that time. Heather is now nursing again in New South Wales.

IAN AND ALINA McKENZIE

Because he had experience in banking, Ian McKenzie had thought of being a missionary accountant in Korea. He had hoped to be sent from his native land of Australia by the Presbyterian Church. However, he accepted the advice of his minister in New South Wales that he should study at the Free Church College in Edinburgh. Before admission there, he qualified for University entrance and graduated in Arts. In 1964, at the Elder Memorial Church, Leith, he was ordained to the ministry and appointed Mission Superintendent of the Free Church Mission in India. He served in that capacity for twenty years. In 1966, Alina Murchison came from Scotland to be married to him in Lakhnadon. She was a daughter of the Alness Schoolhouse, a step-daughter of Professor A. M. Renwick, and had trained as a Health Visitor.

Administration has been a burden for many missionaries, not least for Ian McKenzie. Dr Everard, addressing the Free Church General Assembly in 1974, came to his defence: ".....neither is it right for you to expect an ordained missionary to spend hours of his time doing accounts and other statistics". Later, some of Ian's missionary colleagues, and then an Indian Christian, Mr R. S. Noah, took over office duties.

In 1968, the McKenzies moved from Lakhnadon to Chhapara, where they had closer contact with the School and the Orphanage. There had been a tradition of holding winter camps for evangelism in outlying villages. Instead, in 1969, the McKenzies began camps that catered mainly for children of Christian families, including orphans from Seoni as well as Chhapara. Children of other faiths who attended Sunday School also benefited. Indian Scripture Union workers helped at camp and at Daily Vacational Bible Schools which had become popular during Nan Dunlop's days in Chhapara.

Seeing the Rev. Prakash Kumar well established as minister of the congregation of Chhapara and Lakhnadon, Ian McKenzie determined to leave the mission-compound atmosphere. Alina cooperated wholeheartedly. By 1976 five adolescent orphan boys had outgrown Chhapara Mission School, and Seoni's boarding arrangements were not satisfactory for them. They were accepted in Jabalpur Boys' Christian High School. Missions had an agreement that one would not trespass on the area worked by another mission. This "law of comity", however, did not operate in cities. The McKenzies therefore moved with the lads to Premnagar, a suburb of Jabalpur city, fifty-three miles north of Lakhnadon. A simple Indian-style house was rented, and a young house-father, Francis Masih, employed to be with the boys in their half of the building.

The Rev. David John of Seoni trained in Union Bible Seminary, Yeotmal, and came into Free Church work at Jabalpur in 1979. He ministered first at Vijainagar (another suburb of Jabalpur, about two miles from Premnagar), where Free Church witness had just started. In 1983, he changed places with Ian McKenzie who, for his last year in India, ministered at Vijainagar. At that time the McKenzies lived at Leonard Theological Seminary, where Alina gave nursing services to students and staff in exchange for simple rent-free accommodation.

Christian people of other denominations whose places of worship in Jabalpur city were many miles away were grateful for good ministries close at hand. The gathering together of these two congregations made the setting up of a Presbytery feasible. Ian McKenzie worked towards this but did not see it happen. The need of further education for their three sons led the McKenzies to settle in Glasgow. There, on 18th January 1985, Ian was inducted to Asian Outreach – which is linked to the Grant Street Free Church congregation. An ordained man of Asian background, the Rev. Gurnam Singh, is now in the ministry there. Ian finds fulfilment in personal work among overseas students of many countries, some of which are more or less closed to the Gospel.

Mary Ann MacDonald

Helen Ramsay

Mervyn Oliver

*Flora MacLeod with Kiran
(left) and Vinai (right).*

Ian and Alina McKenzie. The car retained its sticker long after it was sold to a Jabalpur merchant.

Anne Urquhart (left) and Heather Beaton. The mother of the children pictured, Grace Westerduin (neé Allan), is a niece of Dr. Annie Mackay. Her husband worked in a branch of the World Health Organisation. Their home in Dehli (shown here) was a haven for rest and Christian fellowship.

the joy of the Lord

The following account of activities at Lakhnadon in 1960, like that given later of a typical week in 1989, is not taken from a diary but is based on actual happenings.

Sunday: The Rev. Prakash Kumar calls at the hospital at 8.15 a.m., to collect the keys of the church.

Sixteen gather at 8.30 a.m., and twelve at 4 p.m. for the services. He takes a Sunday School with forty noisy children in the vestry immediately after the morning service. Dr Annie Mackay teaches a group of a dozen or so in the sweepers' quarter of the town, while Miss Mary Ann Macdonald has fifteen children of policemen, at the hospital. (The Police Station and Law Courts are close to the hospital.)

Lunch is hardly over when two men appear – a maternity call to a village fourteen miles away. Medicines and instruments are stowed away by Tarabai, who organises a bystander – a relative of an in-patient – to climb on board too. He will guard the jeep from naughty boys. Dr Annie drives the jeep the first ten miles. From there, she rides a bony old horse on a very rough track. Having assessed the patient's condition, she reassures the host of relatives, enlists the help of the most intelligent-looking women, and sets to.

Skill and patience are rewarded. Relaxing while hot, sweet tea is served and while the men find the money to pay for the visit, she talks of the Lord Jesus. One lad who can read accepts a gospel portion. She sings a simple song, a version of the 23rd Psalm, to help them remember God's concern for them. Then they must hurry, because daylight is fading. Instead of the horse, a bullock-cart appears. No relaxing in it, since the road is so rocky.

It's a very weary woman who climbs out of the jeep at Lakhnadon. How many of the doctors who qualified with her are still practising so actively at the age of sixty-seven? Paraffin lamps are lit. At worship together, Mary and she thank God for all his goodness, committing to him all done in his name. Mercifully, the night is quiet.

Monday: Bazaar day in Lakhnadon. It's the minister's day off. His wife, Premlata, is on duty all morning at the Hospital, singing and telling the Christian message to patients and their relatives. There are perhaps eighty people in all, gathered from a wide radius around Lakhnadon.

In the afternoon, Mary, who is housekeeper this month, gives the shopping list to Mahu, the cook: potatoes, onions, tomatoes, lentils, wheat and guavas. A small boy has brought eggs to the back door. She tests them in a bowl of water, bargains cheerfully with him and buys the seven that did not float. She checks the paraffin refrigerator that is smoking dangerously. However much trouble it causes, it is a very welcome piece of equipment provided by dear ladies in Scotland. After seeing stragglers from the morning clinic, Mary has time for a brief visit to the Police Lines – so called simply because the houses are built in straight lines – to see the mothers of her Sunday School children. Then she checks the shopping and the money spent, before attending to in-patients again.

From 3 – 5.30 p.m., Dr Annie mixes with the crowds in the thronging market, distributing tracts, accepting an invitation from one here and one there to sit indoors for a while. A friendly shopkeeper stops lads from letting the air out of her bicycle tyres!

Nan and Helen come from Chhapara for dinner at 6.30 p.m. Then they have a good time of Bible study and prayer, with discussion of mission business. Over supper there's a quick and hilarious game of Scrabble.

Tuesday: At 4 a.m., a call to see an ill child in Lakhnadon. The family agrees to admission. This makes treatment easier but also means a constant stream of relatives in and out. Rich people accustomed to having their own way, they have no inclination to heed requests to limit their visiting. By lunch time, Dr Annie, with good help from Tarabai and Ruthbai, has seen thirty out-patients. Mary has dealt with a twin delivery in the Hospital. Siesta after lunch is welcome. But discipline – self-imposed – is strict, and at 3 p.m. sharp the jeep, plus medicine box and gramophone, is ready.

Tuesday is bazaar day at Kahani. The evangelist, Mr Tiwari, gets out after a few miles. He goes to see a school-master and continues discussion from a previous visit. Tarabai and Mary stop in Kahani. They are well-known here, since camping near the village recently. Demand for scabies ointment and for eye drops is brisk, with plenty of banter over the token payment. The gramophone plays gospel records in a local dialect and attracts quite a crowd. Some listen intently and accept Scripture Gift Mission leaflets.

Rev. Prakash and Dr Annie have gone on the extra eight miles to Ghansore, where the postmaster, who is a Christian, rents the old mission house. His family gathers with a few neighbours while Prakash conducts worship in the home. Roman Catholic influence in the area is discussed. Prakash encourages them to study the Bible daily, with prayer.

On the way back, palm trees against the sunset sky are beautiful.

Wednesday: Rev. Prakash spends the morning in preparation for the mid-week meeting in the church at 4 p.m.

Just after the 7.30 a.m. prayer-time at the hospital, an agitated man hurries in off a lorry that has stopped at the gate. He calls for help for his wife at home, three miles beyond Dhuma. Before long, Dr Annie is at her bedside, which means kneeling on a mud floor beside the cotton mattress. The patient is mother to four living children. Three others have died. The one trying to be born is lying transversely in the womb. The woman has been in labour all night attended by an unqualified midwife, and is now in a desperate state. It would be too dangerous to attempt delivery without facilities for Caesarean section. The relatives agree to transfer her to Jabalpur. After first-aid, she is laid on straw in the back of the jeep and the anxious journey begins. Heavy lorries, reckoning that might is right, often force the jeep off the strip of tarmac. Fortunately, they avoid collision with one stopped on a blind corner of the steep road going down to the Narmada River valley.

Jabalpur's streets are crowded with people, cows, buffaloes and rickshaws, as well as motor traffic. At last they park by The Elgin, an old maternity hospital dating far back to the time of the Raj. A porter recognises the jeep and brings a stretcher at once. What a relief to hand over responsibility to the senior doctor on duty, a tiny lady from South India!

Dr Annie calls at the American Methodist Mission compound where Louise Campbell, a veteran missionary, or her Indian colleague, Pushpa Lall, serves tea whenever tired folk arrive, day or night. Dim coolness in this old house is welcome too, after the glaring heat of the road.

It's 5 p.m. when, after doing shopping for hospital and home, Dr Annie calls at The Elgin again. Her patient is satisfactory, but the babe is dead. Three of the six relatives climb into the jeep. Their company is particularly welcome when the engine gives trouble on a lonely stretch of road. It's good that a torch is standard equipment on a maternity call! The driver of a passing truck fixes a loose wire but won't take payment. Even when the jeep was towed home a month earlier, Dr Annie couldn't persuade her rescuer to accept anything – except a New Testament!

Although the amount of water is rationed, a warm bath in the zinc tub feels very good.

Thursday: *Patients who were disappointed yesterday at not having been seen by the doctor are early in the queue today. Some are impatient with the Biblewoman, Premlata, who talks of Christ while the doctor examines in-patients first. Others are interested in the literature on sale.*

This morning Rev. Prakash is away on his cycle as usual, visiting villages west of Lakhnadon. He finds that most adults are in the fields and has a word with them there. The Master in a government Primary School – a tiny two-roomed building with five classes – knows him from their own school days in Chhapara and invites him to address the children.

Thursday being bazaar day in Dhuma, the jeep leaves promptly at 3 p.m. Today Mary gets off half-way there to renew friendship with families contacted through the Hospital and to remind them of a Saviour's love. Tiwari visits another group of villages.

Relatives of the lady taken to Jabalpur yesterday have come to buy and sell in Dhuma today. They and others listen to the evangelist Mr Godwin Laxman and to Rev. Prakash, who are witnessing together in the busy market. Discussion follows.

Before the jeep returns to Lakhnadon, the Christians gather in Godwin's home for a short time of worship and fellowship.

Mary has a disturbed night. She is up four times to give care to a tiny, ill child. How weary she is when another day dawns! Chronic dysentery as usual saps her energy.

Friday: *Lakhnadon's second market day of the week. Its routine is much as Monday's. Today is a Hindu festival, and larger crowds than usual throng the bazaar. Rev. Prakash and the ladies sell ten gospels and one New Testament, and give out dozens of tracts.*

Saturday: *Rev. Prakash is busy preparing for tomorrow's services. Since today is the last day of the month, all mission workers come for their pay. These days, Dr Annie is the one who sits with the books in which signature or thumb-print is entered. She has to remember the month's happenings. There's a warning for the water-carrier, who was found asleep about 9 a.m. on two occasions; a question for the lad who was on sweeping duties the day his mother was away – doesn't he know he must **not** accept money from patients, even if he has cleaned up a huge mess? There's a fine of two rupees on the washerwoman, because a good bedcover was returned with a six-inch tear and she didn't even mention it.*

Now for the church workers. A younger lady missionary would feel very awkward counting out rupees to – and receiving the signatures of – the under-shepherds of the flock. Then there's the routine of checking log-books – their record of visits to villages and of books sold. It seems so inappropriate, reinforcing the idea that these men of God are "servants of the Mission". At least Dr Annie has seniority on her side!

Four women and Tiwari gather at 4 p.m. at his home on the Toriya to pray for tomorrow's services and for the Sunday Schools. If he had not been preaching at Chhapara last Sunday, this informal meeting would have been Tiwari's only time of fellowship with Christians outwith his own family during the entire week. Does the dear man himself ever regret his vow at baptism never again to set foot in Lakhnadon town? His fellow-believers certainly do.

The rocks of the Toriya reflect the day's heat as Tarabai and the two Scottish women walk down to the hospital. Herds of homeward-bound cattle and goats raise clouds of dust along the road. Children driving the animals, and day-labourers returning to their villages call a cheery greeting. Well-dressed youths speed past on new bicycles. How will they all spend the Lord's Day tomorrow? At the hospital, old Nimabai is waiting to hand over mail collected at the Post Office and to return the church key. On Saturday afternoons she cleans the church building. It's the only time she goes. Ever since she was a young girl, scarcely wanted by her family, she has been a faithful servant with Dr Annie. Not able to read and able to write only her name, she has memorised the Lord's Prayer and songs about his work of salvation. Her life and behaviour give evidence of a saving faith. But there is fear of man too and she has never made a public profession of faith in Christ.

7

No Objection to Return?

New missionaries during the period 1970-88:
**Miss Kathleen Macleod; Dr Donald and Mrs Joan MacDonald;
Miss Barbara Stone; Miss Elizabeth Ferrier;
Miss Marie Christine Lux**

Those who continued:
**Miss Nan Dunlop; Miss Mary Ann Macdonald; Dr Helen Ramsay;
Miss Flora Macleod; Dr Anne Urquhart; Miss Heather Beaton;
Rev. Ian and Mrs Alina McKenzie**

KATHLEEN MACLEOD
Ian McKenzie mentioned Lakhnadon's great need of nurses when he visited
Aberdeen in 1970. Kathleen Macleod of Lewis, a graduate staff-nurse,
offered to go. Having been persuaded that Midwifery skills were essential,
she took that training also. The Board had advertised just then for short-
term workers and Kathleen's intention was to go to India for one or two
years only. Surely sensing her worth, the Chairman persuaded her to accept
a regular four-year contract. At Landour Language School, Kathleen, like
the MacDonalds who followed her, survived the financial hardship of living
in a hill resort where the cost of living was high at a time when the pound
was weak against the rupee.

After her term in India, which was from October 1973, Kathleen studied
at the Bible Training Institute in Glasgow and at Liverpool's School of
Tropical Medicine. Going out again in 1980, she was responsible for
establishing Community Health work in villages around Lakhnadon. Insights
from her Melbost crofting background were useful in that situation, since
the ethos of rural communities is similar the world over. A typical day
meant one stint from 7 a.m. to 12.30 p.m., and another from 4 to 6.30
p.m.; which adds up to only eight hours. But just imagine the fatigue
factor – drive yourself over rocky or dusty roads in a very basic jeep; train
illiterate women to be agents of change; talk (and drink tea) with tradition-
bound mothers-in-law and village headmen; immunise children by the

dozen – and all in intense heat! By the time she resigned – on health grounds – in 1985, that work was firmly in the hands of nationals. Kathleen is now nursing in Stornoway.

DONALD AND JOAN MACDONALD

A month after Kathleen, Dr Donald and Mrs Joan MacDonald came to Lakhnadon. There had been a great burden in prayer among the missionaries there at the time of the 1963 Free Church Youth Conference, held at Nairn. Ian McKenzie was its Convener. We learned years later that Donald MacDonald, a medical student from Kildonan, was influenced then for his eternal good.

During the fifties and sixties, the Edinburgh Missionary Youth Fellowship focused attention on Free Church work abroad. When in 1966 the need for equipment at the enlarged hospital in Lakhnadon became known, Donald organised H.E.L.P. – Hospital Equipment for Lakhnadon Project. In 1970, he married Joan, daughter of the Rev. Alasdair and Mrs MacFarlane of the Kilmuir Free Church manse. Joan had trained in Home Economics. After their marriage they prepared to go to India. Waiting time was well spent in further studies by Donald, who became a Fellow of the Royal College of Surgeons of Edinburgh (F.R.C.S. Ed.).

From 1967, missionaries entering India have required special endorsements on their passports before entry; residential permits, renewable yearly, while staying there; and a "NO OBJECTION TO RETURN" stamp on their passports if they want to go back after leave spent outside India. Restrictions gradually became tighter and few new missionaries were allowed in during the seventies. It is possible that the absence on prolonged sick-leave of Dr Anne Urquhart during 1973 lent weight to the application for Dr MacDonald. The granting of visas to the MacDonalds, to Kathleen Macleod and to Barbara Stone three years later was seen as a specific answer to prayer. With their young son, Donald and Joan arrived at Lakhnadon in November 1973.

The equipment provided for the medical work by H.E.L.P. was soon being used by Donald himself. An appeal made in 1978 for funds to upgrade the hospital further brought in over £22,000. Although shortage of materials caused delay, the new buildings were completed in 1982. During his fifteen years there, it was not necessary for so many patients to go to Jabalpur for surgical treatment. In fact, some travelled from the city to have operations performed at Lakhnadon.

As well as seeing to formalities for registration of Lakhnadon Christian Hospital as a charitable society under the new management of the Emmanuel Hospital Association, Dr MacDonald took seriously his duties in the congregation and Kirk Session. He often preached and led Bible studies in Hindi. Under his guidance, the Psalmody Committee operated effectively. Aware of the preparations necessary for the birth of a Presbytery, Donald, during 1983-84 when sick-leave ran on into home-leave, studied at the Free Church College. He found Pastoral Theology lectures particularly helpful and prepared a simplified version of "The Blue Book" – The Practice of the Free Church of Scotland – for use in India. Back in India, the Church Development Committee worked hard. On 20th September 1986, the Presbytery of the Free Church of Central India was inaugurated. Having resigned from the work in India because of his children's educational needs, Dr MacDonald completed his studies at the Free Church College in Edinburgh and is now minister of Bishopbriggs Free Church.

BARBARA STONE

When Barbara Stone was born, her father was a junior executive in an oil company in London. Influenced by the Rev. Murdo Macleod, then minister of the Free Church congregation in London, he came north to study at the Free Church College. In 1968, he was inducted to the Helmsdale congregation and from there his children attended conferences of the Overseas Missionary Fellowship held in Brora. Those conferences influenced both Barbara and her sister Gillian, who spent four years as a missionary in Peru. Barbara's inclination towards work abroad was strengthened by the addresses on Habakkuk given by the Rev. Ernest Lloyd, a missionary of the Christian Witness to Israel, at the 1975 Free Church Youth Conference.

Having trained in General Nursing and in Midwifery, Barbara went to Lakhnadon in 1976. She served there for twelve years. Incorporation of the medical work into the Emmanuel Hospital Association had heightened awareness of academic qualifications. To fit her better for the post of Nursing Superintendent, Barbara took a course in Nursing Administration while on home leave. Considering the advanced course in London much too expensive, the Foreign Missions' Board accepted Dingwall congregation's offer to pay for a shorter one in Edinburgh. This was quite adequate. Back in India, even with heavy practical and administrative duties, Barbara found time to prepare for and teach her Sunday School class for Hindu children on the *Toriya*, and was encouraged by the interest shown.She resigned in 1988. The following year she married Keith Schmidt, a widower and a member of the Presbyterian Church of Eastern Australia in Brisbane.

ELIZABETH FERRIER

Indian Government restrictions limited Elizabeth Ferrier's time of missionary service to only two years. Daughter of the Rev. Hugh and Mrs Ferrier of the Free North Manse, Inverness, she became interested in India through contact with missionaries visiting the home and through reading books. Elizabeth is a graduate nurse with Midwifery training. She visited Lakhnadon privately for three months in 1980-81 and for three weeks in 1982, before volunteering for long-term service in 1983. Because it was considered that the Bible and Medical Missionary Fellowship (B.M.M.F.) was more likely to secure her entry to India, she went under the auspices of that organisation. After the assassination of Prime Minister Indira Gandhi in 1984, restrictions on all foreigners tightened, and Elizabeth was given notice to leave the country. B.M.M.F. asked that she be relocated to their work in Pakistan but the Foreign Missions' Board pointed out that they had no mandate to allow that, and she returned to nursing in Edinburgh. She is now on the Personnel Committee of the Scottish branch of Interserve, as B.M.M.F. is now called. In 1986 Elizabeth married Calum Ferguson, an accountant at the Free Church Offices and an elder of Livingston Free Church.

MARIE CHRISTINE LUX

Marie Christine Lux is Belgian and of Roman Catholic background. She came to a personal faith in Christ during nursing training in Tasmania. While a student midwife in Edinburgh, she became a member of St Columba's Free Church. Not having grown up in a home where Christ was honoured as Saviour, Marie Christine finds his love very, very wonderful. Concern for poor people dates from her childhood in what was then the Belgian Congo. So she considers it natural for her to be a missionary, now that she is a Christian.

While her application for a visa for India was being processed, she was in Somalia with TEAR Fund, the Evangelical Alliance's relief agency. When she went to India in 1982, it was with a three-month visa, which was renewed only once. After even such a short time, her roots had gone remarkably deep. Aware of her need for more preparation for Christian service, she attended the Bible Training Institute in Glasgow for one year. Then followed two years in the Andes of Peru, encouraging better health and hygiene among isolated villagers. Now that there is less need for expatriate nurses in Peru, she has gone to the Central African Republic, again under TEAR Fund – but seconded by the Free Church. There she is seeking to establish Community Health work in a remote jungle area. Warm love to God and man; sensitivity, very evident in her writing and drawings; stickability; and, not least, a wonderful sense of humour are some of the qualities that make Marie Christine welcome in any continent.

Kathleen MacLeod checking village children for malnutrition.

Donald and Joan MacDonald and family.

Barbara Stone

Elizabeth Ferrier

Marie Christine Lux

kaleidoscope

In May 1984, Mrs Joan MacDonald, wife of Dr Donald MacDonald, addressed ladies at a W.F.M.A. meeting in Edinburgh. Here is part of her talk.

What have I heard? A lot of music for a start. Much of it is rubbishy, film pop music. It's not that we willingly lend our ears to it. It invades our homes and our ears and even our minds without invitation. Electricity has brought many benefits but it has also brought the scourge of amplifiers and loudspeakers. Nowadays the local bands can be supplemented by records and tapes, and celebration music can be shared by neighbours within a wide radius whether they want it or not. This is particularly wearing on the nerves at festival times and at the wedding season in May. Some nights perhaps more than ten loudspeakers can be blaring at the same time, all from different functions.

Sometimes the local temple has its loudspeakers pouring forth Hindu scriptures in the sing-song voice of the priest. This is a continuous 24-hour affair and can last many weeks. The weather is so hot that the windows have to be kept open and there is no way of shutting out the noise. To prevent the children from falling asleep with this rubbish seeping into their subconscious, I sang them to sleep with psalms or hymns – a practice I still continue with the younger ones. Sometimes an electricity cut seemed like an answer to prayer – at least it effectively silenced the loudspeakers. It also meant that the overhead fans went off, and I was not only singing the children to sleep but fanning them with a hand fan and fetching drinks of iced water. Inside temperatures at that time of night can be about 95°F in the hot weather. Our minds need the Lord's protection at such times.

I have heard children: children playing; children laughing; children singing. My own children and their friends all speaking fluent Hindi. No language barrier there. Children squabbling; children crying; children praying, which is hallowed ground. Ill children whimpering in hospital beds; and mothers wailing over the loss of yet another child through an illness, often caused by dirty water supplies. When someone dies in the hospital, relatives immediately begin wailing. It is a solemnising sound, and empty of hope.

I've heard happy sounds at the hospital too: laughter and joy at a live birth; and flowery speeches of thanks to staff for their skill and caring. There are quiet sounds: the doves; and the wind rustling the ripened wheat in the hospital farm.

Then there are the travelling sounds, which to me are more evocative of India than anything else. The hustle and bustle, shouting and shoving of an Indian railway station have to be seen and heard to be believed. Tea and coffee sellers try to interest us in some unpalatable brew at 5.30 a.m. as, patiently sitting out our wait for a late train, we idly watch fat railway rats playing on the lines. There's the whine of beggars and the persistent niggling of tired, hot and irritable children and adults. There's the thud of one's heart as the train looms into the station.

There's a flat, strained, little, little voice, "Goodbye, Mum and Dad; see you at mid-term," and the scream of the whistle as the train rushes off, carrying the children a thousand miles away to school. And there is the silent weeping and the silent prayer that only God hears.

I love bazaar days: hearing folk talk as they pass the house; the sound of oxen bells and the creak of wooden carts and the barking of dogs.

There are the frightening sounds: of political processions, chanting nasty slogans; thunderstorms and high winds; voices raised in anger and bitterness; screams of beaten children or maybe of some hysterical person.

There is the comforting murmur of shared prayer in fellowship meetings, and the happy laughter of relaxed friendship.

What have I seen? I have seen poverty. I have seen the reality of poverty. Poverty is not a conscience-pricking photograph. Poverty has a face and an emaciated body. Poverty is people, people I know. Individuals whom God has created with a right to human dignity. Poverty robs a working man of the enjoyment of his food, for, when one meal is eaten, there is no knowledge of where the next one is coming from. Poverty robs a woman of real joy in marriage and family – hard, labouring jobs to earn money for essentials drain her strength and, in spite of the extra income, children still die through lack of medical care.

Poverty robs a community of tranquillity because the rich exploit the defenceless poor.

We have known women come into hospital with terrible obstetric complications. Women being left to die, because it's cheaper to get another wife than to pay for medical care.

People who live in shanty towns are thankful they are not on the pavements and under bridges, or living in cold corners as so many, many are. I have seen naked children literally playing in the gutter. Such devastating, degrading poverty, what can one do in the face of it? After ten years in India I cannot come to terms with it, and I hope I never will.

The eyes dwell sympathetically on friends and colleagues whose faces reflect the utter exhaustion they feel after a long, sustained period of hard work. It is especially hard on nurses who have a husband and family to care for as well as a demanding job.

Of spiritual deprivation I have said nothing. Witnessing open idol worship is a shocking experience. To see a man prostrate himself before a grotesque, painted, stone figure, kiss its feet and lovingly adorn it with flowers makes me realise the darkness that Satan has cast over the minds of idol worshippers. These people are in deadly earnest, seeking spiritual truth. We never allow our children to mock them, as they may be inclined to do. Will you pray for such people, that God will provide his servants with a key to unlock these bound minds?

What of your minds? Are they confused by the kaleidoscope of images presented to you? If they are, then you have really identified with those who work in this situation.

III   THREE STRANDS OF SERVICE

'Serve one another in love.' [Gal. 5.13]

8
Motherless Bairns

At sunset on 16th February 1927, a small girl was crying her heart out at the Chhapara bus-stop. She and her two brothers were being taken to Seoni by men they did not know. For eighteen months, since their mother had died, they had been cared for in the home of the Rev. Evan and Mrs Eva Mackenzie at Lakhnadon. They had been happy there. And now they were most unhappy. It was a sad ending to what had started in great hope.

But what else could Mr Mackenzie expect? His report to Scotland in 1926 had said: "The Orphanage – so far we have only three children. Our hope is that 'the little one may become a thousand'." But Hindus resented what they saw as colonial and Christian greed for poor children. Mr Mackenzie had not adopted that family legally. A Hindu Society challenged his right to have them and the judge in Seoni ordered that they be handed over, and so tears flow. An incident like that sticks in the memory, collective as well as personal.

Two years later, Dr Willie Urquhart was asked to take charge of another family, of four orphans. The Foreign Missions' Committee in Edinburgh was consulted. **"Legal advice must be taken."** We do not hear of these four orphans again.

In the meantime, the Urquharts' own firstborn arrived. Housekeeping for the young mother involved many vital things, such as the careful boiling of drinking water and of buffalo milk. The Hindu nursemaid who had looked after those three orphan children for eighteen months was employed to help. Her name, Shanti, means peace. Six months after the birth of a second son, recurrent malaria threatened Dr Urquhart's life, and his self-medication with high doses of quinine brought complications. His service in India was complete in four years. Shanti, intrigued by his fatherly concern to teach his boys to pray before food and at bedtime, received God's peace in her heart. Into her care in 1932 came one tiny girl, Jaiwanti, given to the busy Scottish lady-missionaries when her mother died. Legal adoption papers were in order for her and for an older girl Surajmukhi, who was sent to school at Seoni. The Free Church Orphanage in India was established. Or so it seemed.

But not until 1955 was the Orphanage accepted as part of the official policy of the Foreign Missions' Committee. In 1941 the Rev. David Mackenzie was appointed Convener of that Committee. His annual reports indicate clearly that he was concerned that the Orphanage work should be on a sounder footing. The Rev. Duncan Leitch, who became Vice-Convener in 1943 and later Convener, shared this concern. Over almost all of the next twelve years, one or other of these men was Convener. So why the delay of twenty-three years in the official acceptance of this work?

As in other matters, shortage of money was one factor. Also, it may have been thought that immorality would be encouraged. Yet the vast majority of children taken into care were victims of maternal mortality, not the products of immorality. A third factor was probably the main one. It seems that the Foreign Missions' Committee, in spite of reassurances from the field, dreaded a repetition of legal action. Elizabeth Macleod in 1944 and Dr Jeannie Grant, a guest speaker from Seoni in 1947, told the Fathers and Brethren met in General Assembly at Edinburgh of the advantages of orphanage work as a training-ground for future workers. A mission without national workers was like a man without hands, they said. And there would be trouble in securing good workers until we supplied our own, either from the Orphanage or from Christian families. But still there was delay.

The children being cared for before 1955 were not aware of their unofficial status – unofficial as far as the Committee in Edinburgh was concerned.

As early as 1905, when Miss Elizabeth Macleod joined the Original Secession Mission work in Seoni, congregations in the Free Church began adopting individual children. In 1906 Buccleuch and Greyfriars Sabbath School sent £5, the amount then needed for one year's support for an Indian child. Their boy was named Gordon McAlister, after the congregation's two senior ministers. Kirkcaldy sent £5 the following year. Clothes and toys for the children in Seoni were despatched year after year by ladies in Scotland.

During the first two decades of the twentieth century, the Seoni Orphanage had grown rapidly in times of famine or epidemic illness. In 1914 Mr McNeel was in charge of four out of eight plague camps in the district. Government officials regularly brought orphans to him from outlying areas. During the influenza pandemic of 1918, thirty more children were accepted.

Soon after the Free Church restarted her own mission work in 1924, the Seoni court ruling mentioned above occurred. Those three orphans were removed from the Mackenzies' care. From then on, the Foreign Missions' Committee did not oppose support of individual children but they would not take responsibility for the Orphanage as a matter of policy. Collecting boxes of the Foreign Missions' Association in 1927 carried a picture of Surajmukhi. In 1929 the Committee refused to allow "The Instructor" to publish a letter from the wife of Dr Willie Urquhart, because it referred to "an extension of work not authorised by the committee". We do not have that letter but it probably concerned the need for well-organised support of orphans. Dr Annie Mackay's annual report included in "The Monthly Record" of May 1932 told of orphanage work that was not a charge on mission funds. The infant Jaiwanti's picture appeared in "The Instructor" at the time of the Rev. Murray Macleod's going to India in 1933.

Like his missionary colleagues, Murray Macleod was in no doubt about the benefits of orphanage work. Unlike them, he was outspoken. He let the Committee know that he considered the Orphanage an essential part of missionary work. The Committee advised him that they considered it "not expedient", and forbade it as policy. His wife cared for motherless infants brought by distraught fathers. Many whose health was precarious did not survive.

Lena Gillies remembers how, early one morning at Lakhnadon in 1934, her Hindi lesson was interrupted by the arrival of a man with his tiny, weak child. Her teacher named him on the spot – Prakash Kumar, "prince of light". He was cared for by Mrs Sarah Macleod before their own first child was born. Later, St George's congregation in Sydney supported him. This became the pattern. In 1938 Dr Annie Mackay had just taken responsibility for a baby boy when St Columba's congregation in Edinburgh asked if they might adopt a child in memory of their late minister, Dr Alexander Stewart. And so Alexander's support was assured. Not all the children were received soon after birth – domestic tragedy sometimes brought them at older ages as a family group.

The name Alexander is familiar in India from the exploits of Alexander the Great. The practice of naming orphans after people in Scotland soon died out and most Free Church mission children have names that are locally acceptable. Dayal Masih means "Christ is merciful". Vinodh Das means "servant of gladness". The custom of having a chosen first name followed by the family name, while not uniform in Eastern society, is common in Christian communities of North India. Since missionaries were usually in charge of the orphans, giving one's guardian's name when applying, for example, for a place in college, might be awkward. Macleod and McKenzie are unfamiliar to most English- as well as Hindi-speakers in India. Dunlop is identified with vehicle tyres, and Ramsay may be written down as Ram Singh!

The General Assembly of 1939 was informed that the care of orphans was being financed not by mission funds but by individual congregations in Australia and Scotland. But we will never know how much missionaries themselves gave! Details of the ten children in care were given in "The Monthly Record" of July 1940. So, by 1940, the Free Church of Scotland was well aware that in Central India, from the eight hundred villages for whose evangelism she was responsible, motherless boys and girls were coming into her fold. The *ad hoc* arrangement was – and after 1955 continued to be – satisfactory as far as individual support was concerned. Sponsorship by congregations has the advantage of particular interest in and particular prayer for each child. But matters of general concern, such as accommodation and the need for suitable full-time staff, could be given only scant attention.

Accommodation in the 1930s and 1940s was in small houses on the *Toriya*, Lakhnadon, at a respectable distance behind the Big Bungalow. Perhaps colonial attitudes unconsciously approved this position? Although cramped inside, there was enormous scope out-of-doors on that five-acre site. The Rev. Prakash Kumar remembers his early childhood there as a happy time. Mrs Gajaribai Lall, an earnest Christian lady who was separated from her husband in Nagpur, was employed as matron. She and her daughter Tarabai, a Nursery School teacher, cared for and taught the children, with Shanti as faithful cook and helper. When the little church was built in Lakhnadon village in 1935, Murray Macleod rejoiced, "Now our children will be able to go to church!"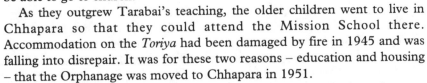

As they outgrew Tarabai's teaching, the older children went to live in Chhapara so that they could attend the Mission School there. Accommodation on the *Toriya* had been damaged by fire in 1945 and was falling into disrepair. It was for these two reasons – education and housing – that the Orphanage was moved to Chhapara in 1951.

There, a tiny house and a shed, which had housed bullocks and a cart, were reconstructed. Shanti continued as cook. She died in 1961. Gajaribai was succeeded by a widow, Mrs Rahilbai Patrick. She, with her late husband, a teacher, had transferred from Secession to Free Church Mission employment in Chhapara in 1924. Rahilbai, known as Bari Mama, "great mother", had been trained to give out medicines by Dr Jeannie Grant in Seoni. For many years she dispensed medicines at Chhapara and mothered the orphan children, teaching the girls the elements of house-keeping.

Disciplining the boys was more difficult, especially as she grew older. There was no foster-father until the Rev. Prakash Kumar and his wife Premlata took over responsibility after their move from Lakhnadon to Chhapara in 1965. But, from the earliest days, a very important contribution was made by Charan Masih. After he became a Christian, he was trained by Elizabeth Macleod and was employed as a cook to missionaries in Chhapara for four decades. Even more important than his skills as a cook was his quiet wise counsel in all matters concerning the children, who called him "Papa". He loved them dearly. With his friend Mukharam, a Hindu house-servant, he helped tirelessly to care for them. Charan died in 1969. Then Mukharam's loyalty waned.

Since the Mission's Middle School at Chhapara had been discontinued in 1940, children over Primary School age went away to Boarding Schools of other Christian missions – in Seoni, Chhindwara (forty miles west of Seoni, where Swedish Lutherans worked) or Jabalpur. Hostel life was not always very happy and the youngsters were glad to come home for holidays. After the Government High School opened in Chhapara in 1957, some of them attended it.

For three months during the winter of 1954-55, the first-ever twentieth century delegate to India of the Free Church Foreign Missions' Committee, its Convener, the Rev. Duncan Leitch, and his wife visited Lakhnadon. Part of his report that had reference to the orphans was as follows:

"These points should be noted:
1. There are fourteen orphans at different stages being supported by us.
2. All these children have been legally adopted according to Indian law, a relative or guardian in each case witnessing before a police official that he or she is willing to hand over the child to the Mission.
3. It is reckoned that £24 is the average sum required to maintain a child. The total required in 1955 on this basis will be £336. In 1954, £291 was contributed by congregations for Orphanage work. The Financial Statement for the year ending December 1954 appears to indicate that if the Orphanage is officially recognised by the Church it will not be a charge on Mission funds. The income was Rs 4,560 (rupees); expenditure Rs 4,476.
4. Miss Brown is presently in charge of the orphans and has the assistance

of a matron, who is also employed as a dispenser, and of a cook.

5. Of the orphans who have been brought up by us none has gone back to Hinduism. Four have professed faith in Christ and have been baptised. At present, three are teachers (two untrained); one is in training as an evangelist and another as a nurse.

6. Though the work is not without disappointments and difficulties, it does appear to offer a fruitful sphere of Christian service. The children are being well cared for and trained in the way of the Lord.

Recommendations:

1. In view of the foregoing facts it is recommended that the Assembly be asked to give its official approval of the orphan work.

2. Having regard to the uncertain future of Christian Missions in India, it is recommended that, in no circumstances, should more children be received; and that only the General Assembly have power to reverse this finding.

3. Although the present accommodation is limited, in view of the fact that several of the orphans will be leaving us in the next two years, it is not recommended that larger premises be acquired."

The Finding of the 1955 General Assembly relating to India included the following:

"They receive the report of the Convener on the India Mission and instruct the Committee to give effect to the recommendations contained therein.

They request the Committee to take the oversight of the Indian Orphanage; in view, however, of the uncertain future of Christian Missions in India they instruct that no more children be received."

It could be said that in these lines we see the beginning and, simultaneously, the end of the Free Church Orphanage in India.

But, as it was not the real beginning, so neither was it the real end. To legislate in Edinburgh was one thing; to harden one's heart against tiny

Bari Mama   *Papa*

motherless infants in Chhapara another. Many **were** turned away and the relatives were directed to larger institutions in Seoni or Chhindwara. Whether they actually went is another question. Then, in December 1958, Nan Dunlop and Helen Ramsay wavered.

A young Gondh couple had refused stubbornly to stay at the Chhapara Dispensary for even one night, although warned that the woman's first pregnancy was moving to a dangerous climax. Their twin daughters were born at home. The mother died. The father had to work in the fields all day and there was no-one to look after them. He brought them to Nan and Helen, who began to care for them.

What to do? The political situation was no worse than in 1955. The Field Council referred the matter to the Foreign Missions' Committee, hoping for a sympathetic response. The 1959 General Assembly granted the Committee's request to approve their adoption. From that time, until the very last of eight more children was adopted in 1969, successive General Assemblies noted the additions to the orphan family without referring to the finding of the 1955 Assembly that no more children were to be adopted.

In 1955 the matter of better accommodation for the Orphanage had been set aside, although Dr Annie Mackay had pled for it when in Scotland in 1954. But there was no denying the need when, in 1966, six toddlers left the lady-missionaries' immediate care in Chhapara and moved across the back garden to be with Prakash and Premlata! Flora Macleod drew attention to this need during her home-leave in 1968. The challenge was given by the Foreign Missions' Board to the Women's Foreign Missionary Association. As a result, a new building was erected on what had been waste ground not far from other mission property. On Tuesday 30th September 1969 there was great excitement as the children took possession of their brand new home.

Following the visit to India in 1972 of two delegates from the home Board, the Indian Orphans' Future Support Fund was set up in Scotland and the money invested in India. This was to ensure material provision for the younger children even if (as seemed likely) the Government might restrict the inflow of funds from abroad. From the late 1950s, loans had been granted to the older orphans as they married, to help with housing. Appreciation of the care given to the children by the Rev. Prakash Kumar and his wife was heightened in 1974 when he visited Scotland. They were later given financial aid to build a house for themselves, on condition that it would be home to the orphans too for as long as necessary. This condition is being honoured.

Ian and Alina McKenzie, who had shared the care of the orphans with Prakash and Premlata during their years in Chhapara (1967–75), moved to Jabalpur after home-leave in 1976. Five teenage orphan boys went with them for secondary schooling in the city. At that time, there was word that the old Dispensary site at Chhapara would be flooded when a government dam was completed. Since the Orphanage building was now under-used, in 1981 the medical work was transferred there. It was adapted, extended and opened as Chhapara Christian Health Centre in 1982. There is some lingering hurt among the young people who feel they have lost their home! However, small plots of mission land are now being allocated to the young men and financial help is being arranged for construction of individual homes. While loyal to one another within the joint family of the Orphanage, each appreciates this opportunity of having a place to call his own.

Although no child has been received into the Orphanage since 1969, the influence of the work done persists. It is painfully true that some children have gone far away from Christian fellowship, and that, for some, marriage has brought grief. Yet the church today in Chhapara, and to a lesser extent in Lakhnadon, has grown basically from the Orphanage, as Christian families have now been established.

Volumes could be written if we were to trace in detail the history of each of those cared for. The children might talk of happy (and some not-so-happy!) times at home, at camp or on holiday with a missionary family at one of India's hill-stations; and of solemn impressions made during times of worship at home, in church or at a conference. Missionaries would mention anxiety when infants were seriously ill; joy at steady progress made; concern to ensure suitable training after school; even greater concern for marriage arrangements; and the under-girding faith that God was guiding. Indian helpers could tell amusing tales of foreigners' language mistakes and the children's quick correction of them; of patience exercised until a missionary realised that **her** way of organising things was not the best in an Indian context; and of the solid comfort of knowing that God is faithful.

What about orphans since 1969?

Because Indian Christians are reluctant to adopt and government restrictions on foreign personnel and money have become tight, the ban – on accepting children – imposed by the 1955 General Assembly of the Free Church of Scotland has been strictly enforced since 1969. Maternal mortality has decreased, so far fewer children are left motherless. The distance from Lakhnadon and Chhapara to the nearest Christian Orphanage now makes people reluctant to take an infant away so far, even if help is given with travel arrangements. A few wealthy land-owners in the local Muslim community are glad to adopt any known to be in need.

what kind of love!

In 1979, Alina McKenzie went to Bhopal to make enquiries about further education for Sharan, one of the orphans. Returning, she boarded the night train for Jabalpur.

"Oh good, I've got the top bunk in a ladies' sleeper. I'll get settled down quickly."

*There are already two ladies occupying the lower bunks. They ask the usual general questions – what they consider essential information – destination, purpose of journey, husband's work and pay, number of children (how many **boys?**). I get my sheet and pillow out. It's great to stretch out, despite the hardness of the berth's wooden slats.*

Above the noise of the fans I can hear the women talking. They are from Bhilai, a large industrial city in M.P. They're speaking about Chhapara now.

"That's where the missionaries look after orphans as if they were their very own! My neighbour told me about her childhood there. Her mother died when she was born. The Granny wanted to try to keep her alive – you know how they dip a rag in a seashell filled with goat's milk and make the baby suck it. But her father knew she wouldn't survive that way. He must have been a determined man because he ignored his mother's objections. He took his baby girl to the Mission at Chhapara – or was it at Lakhnadon in those days? The ladies took her in and cared for her. I think there were about a dozen children. You should hear my neighbour Kripa tell how they were cared for! She says that if each one had been the child of those foreigners they would not have been better looked after. It's not that they had a lot of expensive things like toys and fancy clothes. No, it's the memory of the tremendous mother-love that stays with her....."

I lay on my bunk and praised God for this Hindu woman's testimony to the love and care of the missionaries of the past.

"Their works do follow them....."

9

Schools and Schoolmasters

Formal education has been part and parcel of Christian missions in India right through the twentieth century. The vast bureaucratic network set up by the British is an attractive sphere of employment, towards which education is a first step. Hinduism's caste system tends to down-grade manual skills. But the primary motivation of Christian education is that God's revelation in his Word demands hearers, and readers.

In March 1900, John McNeel of Seoni sent a young Indian man to stay at Chhapara. Daniel Cameron was an orphan who had been trained as a catechist. On 17th June 1901, he opened a modest school there, with twenty-one boys enrolled. Soon Jugal Kishore, Chhapara's chief landlord, gifted one acre of ground and on it he built, at his own expense, "a neat commodious building". There, in 1905, thirty-nine boys enrolled in Primary and fifteen in Middle School. Standards of teaching fluctuated over the next two decades.

When the Free Church set up her own mission in 1924, the Rev. Evan MacKenzie advised closing the Chhapara School and opening instead "a first-class one at Lakhnadon, where future agents could be trained". But the local initiative that provided the first school building in Chhapara is an indication of the goodwill there which continues down to the present day. Lakhnadon did have a mission school, but only briefly, from 1901 to 1903. And, through the thirties and forties, the orphan children were taught at the *Toriya,* the hill-top home of the Mission in Lakhnadon. At out-stations, such as Ghansore, twenty-one miles east of Lakhnadon, catechists taught children informally.

In 1926, the Government Inspector declared Chhapara's Mission School buildings and teachers substandard. The teachers were sent to Seoni for upgrading of their skills and on return were supervised by Miss Elizabeth Macleod. She, like most of the missionaries who became Managers of the School in later years, had had no training as a teacher! Dr Annie Mackay on home-leave in Scotland and Dr Willie Urquhart at Landour Language School in 1927 both pled for a higher standard of teaching and accommodation, and especially for a male missionary teacher. A sub-committee was appointed by the Foreign Missions' Committee in Edinburgh to formulate educational policy in India. As a result the General Assembly of May 1928 was advised to order closure of Chhapara Middle School.

Just at that time, a majority of Free Church Presbyteries in Scotland had approved a large loan to build a new school in Lima. Dr Alexander Stewart pled successfully for the "solitary ewe lamb" of Chhapara, and a legacy of £1000 became available. In 1929 a suitable site – the present one – was acquired for £33 "from a private source". In 1930, after some difficulty over a right-of-way, the purpose-built Middle School was opened. It is still in use today.

Staffing continued to be a problem. As well as the veteran Elizabeth Macleod, three younger ladies – Lena Gillies, Edith and Anna Stewart – were also interested in education. The other new missionary of the thirties, the Rev. Murray Macleod, considered that the failure of the home church to send a qualified male teacher to Chhapara, plus the difficulty of recruiting satisfactory Indian staff, warranted closure. **"Don't let the school drift!"** he warned the Foreign Missions' Committee in 1935. By 1939 his colleagues in Lakhnadon and Chhapara had come round to his point of view and the Committee agreed. Thus, because of lack of good teachers, the Middle School was discontinued in 1940.

This meant improved conditions for the Primary School, for which the 1930 building became available.

Munshiram Tiwari, a converted Brahman priest who had been baptised in 1945, was a respected teacher during his four years in Chhapara

(1948–52). Nan Dunlop and Janette Brown, who arrived in 1944 and 1947 respectively, each contributed in her own distinctive way to the life of the school. Babs Sutherland, a graduate teacher, was too busy with her own children to give much time to the Mission School but her enthusiasm for education was evident in the articles she contributed to church magazines.

Some Muslim and Hindu teachers gave good service. There was genuine regret on the part of children, parents and missionaries when Shiv Dayal Singh retired in 1964 after many years as Headmaster. A younger teacher, Pathak, who stepped up to take his place, died in 1973.

The Rev. Prakash Kumar was then appointed Acting Headmaster, but his lack of professional qualifications led to objections being raised in the Government Education Department, from whom a grant is received. After ten years' service as a teacher, Alexander John was appointed Headmaster in 1975 and continues in that position today.

Early schooling for Alexander was on the *Toriya*, with lessons from Tarabai. (It must have seemed strange to both of them when, after her many years' service as compounder at Lakhnadon Hospital, she later taught Kindergarten classes in Chhapara under Alexander!) He left school as soon as possible, but George Sutherland reported in 1957 that Alexander was his apprentice, learning many useful things and might one day be a mason. The following year he was keen to study again. By 1963 he was a student at Jabalpur University, and from there he has not looked back. In addition to his degrees – M.A., B.Comm., B.Ed. – he has a reputation as a writer of magazine articles and short stories. Out of a total of four hundred thousand teachers in Madhya Pradesh in 1984, Alexander and one other man were nominated by Government Inspectors for special awards for excellence in their profession.

A teacher visiting from Edinburgh in 1986 commented about the school: "Behaviour was excellent and there was a fine happy spirit about the place. Mr Alex is obviously a most efficient Headmaster. He has a fine, upright bearing and a quiet confidence which, I should think, inspires pupils and teachers to give of their best. The school has an excellent reputation and there is great competition to get into it."

Alexander is not the only teacher from among the orphans. As early as 1954, Peter joined the staff of the school. At first untrained, he was sponsored for a year at college in 1957. His wife Lila, who had trained before marriage, was appointed in 1958. So each has given more than thirty years' service. Other orphans, and more recently their children, were also brought on to the staff.

Public demand that Chhapara Mission School be reinstated as a Middle School, not only Primary, was voiced in 1964. The Foreign Missions'

Board turned down the request because the medical work was expanding at that time and the political situation was uncertain. The demand was finally heeded in the eighties. By then, children of local Christian families were qualifying as teachers, so giving hopes of adequate staffing. Additional classrooms, financed by a special effort in fund-raising by ladies in Scotland, were declared open by Nan Dunlop when she revisited India in March 1988. In August 1988 there were 568 children enrolled in the school (326 boys and 242 girls), an average of seventy in each class. It is expected that the Middle School will be functioning fully again in 1990. The school will then comprise Kindergarten, five years of Primary and three years of Middle. Several of these years have two classes because of the large number of pupils.

The teacher-visitor in 1986, who was Mrs Doreen Boyd, wife of the Foreign Missions' Board Secretary, commented on various aspects of school life:

"The Kindergarten class with forty-eight pupils sit on the floor in straight lines, on strips of jute carpeting. Modern teaching aids, an abacus and counting blocks, were pointed out. Blackboards are areas on the wall painted black. The children use slates and paper. Reading books are written in Hindi. The quality of print and paper reminded me of the wartime economy books available in my childhood. Most of the teaching is done by rote – with such huge classes there could be little scope for activity methods!

Subjects taught are: reading, writing, arithmetic, Hindi language, history, geography, science, art, drama, music, drill and Religious Education. They learn the Catechism. English is taught in the last class. There is no teacher of remedial subjects; but, if the pupils fall behind, the parents can pay someone to do coaching in the evenings. Ninety per cent of the children wear school uniform and this seems to apply all over India, even in small villages. School starts at 10 a.m. and finishes at 3.45 p.m., except on Saturday when there is early school: 8 – 10.30 a.m.

Mr Alex told the story of the Good Samaritan. A group of children came forward to dramatise the story. They were great actors. Dressed up, with beards and whiskers painted on their faces, they obviously entered into the characters of those whom they portrayed. The Good Samaritan, complete with first-aid kit and water-bottle, was marvellous. With twinkling eyes he bandaged up the victim."

The impressions of another teacher, Miss Mary Gillies, visiting in 1988, were in a similar vein. She found Alexander to be a very worried man; partly because of over-conscientious and frequent visits by government inspectors; and partly because delays in payment of government grants often mean that he cannot pay the teachers on time. As a founding-member of one of the Teachers' Support Groups in Scotland, she encourages us to help improve resources such as books and audio-visual aids, and to promote in-service training of teachers. She reminds us that involvement in the Chhapara School is both an awesome responsibility and a wonderful opportunity, calling for vision and commitment from Christians in Scotland as well as in India. Through the Support Groups, Free Church teachers and other interested friends now take a practical interest in Chhapara School, as well as in educational work in Peru and Southern Africa.

Until recently the Indian Field Council was responsible for managing the school. In 1988 the Free Church Mission Education Society, its members all national Christians, was formally registered with the Indian government authorities.

Alexander John, Headmaster

a policeman remembers

Dr Helen Ramsay recounted the following story in 1984:

Many years ago, Miss Dunlop and I met a young policemen in Jabalpur when I had parked our car too near a corner. He recognised Miss Dunlop and told us that he had attended our Mission School and remembered the Scripture lessons there. He also had had contact in his village with the Rev. Murray Macleod, had played with his sons and heard more of the Gospel. After some years he started having a recurrent dream in which he saw Christ on the cross. He decided he had to find out more about this one who he felt was calling him. His family had moved to another area and he went to a Lutheran church there, had teaching and was baptised. His father put him out of the house and family, but eventually he had got admission to the Police Force and was continuing in the Christian faith.

Stories like that are not common, but there may be others which we have never heard. Certain it is that our Mission Primary School has had a beneficial effect on this area. For a long time it was the only primary school and the manners, discipline and friendliness of those who attended it made the Chhapara area a pleasant one for missionaries and Indian Christians alike. Now that there are two other big Government primary schools the difference in attitudes is sometimes painfully apparent. There is tremendous potential for good through the work and witness of the school.

10
Prevention and Cure at Chhapara

As with Education, so with Medicine – in the face of great need it has been considered a **must** for Christian missions in the twentieth century. Of the total of twenty-five missionaries sent by the Free Church of Scotland to India this century, twenty were diaconal workers, the majority of them nurses or doctors.

From 1900, Indian Christian workers in Chhapara helped sick people as they were able. Their training in Seoni had included elementary health matters. The 14th of December 1925 marked the beginning of the Free Church's medical ministry, after her own Mission was re-established. On that Monday morning seven patients came to the verandah of Dabbu Patail's home in the centre of Chhapara village. He, a wealthy Muslim, rented out part of his house to Elizabeth Macleod and Annie Mackay, who had moved from Seoni four days before.

There was little privacy at Dabbu Patail's and it was a relief when the mission house was repaired. Another small house became available for dispensary work, in the goldsmiths' quarter of the village, very near the bazaar. Rented at first, it was later bought, along with enough adjacent land to give parking for bullock carts (and for a car, when that luxury came). Mr McNeel gave help with necessary alterations, as he had at the ladies' dwelling house. For over thirty years, much good was done from this unpretentious place of healing.

In 1957 further improvements were made so that four mothers and their newborn babies could be accommodated. Facilities for out-patients were made more adequate. Even so, conditions continued primitive. Construction of a large dam at Bhimgarh, about ten miles east of Chhapara, began in the 1970s. Government authorities advised that, when the dam would be in use, the river Wainganga's high-water level would approach the old Dispensary.

On 2nd January 1981 that building ceased to function as a Dispensary or Health Centre. The medical work moved to the 1969 Orphanage building, which was adapted and extended. This brought the work closer to the main road and to staff housing. Chhapara's centre of gravity had itself shifted over the years in that same direction. New buildings for business and housing had been put up on both sides of National Highway Seven, the trunk road that in earlier days had merely skirted the village. When I walked by the old Dispensary in August 1988 there was a sad "For Sale" notice on its wall. Rented out to an immigrant South Indian family who make tin trunks from old tar drums, it was still a hive of industry.

So much for the buildings connected with health care in Chhapara. What about staff and their activities?

Dr Annie Mackay stayed in Chhapara for two years from 1925. After her return from Scotland in 1928, she was usually based in Lakhnadon, visiting Chhapara regularly on a Tuesday (while she remained the only doctor) and at other times as necessary. Rahilbai, trained in Seoni as dispenser and Biblewoman, was helper in Chhapara Dispensary for many years. Christian nurses, expatriate and national, often with no doctor available, have brought relief to countless people in their own homes as well as in the Dispensary. Midwifery practice in the slums of Glasgow, Edinburgh or Belfast was good preparation! Mrs Taramoni Lall, now Sister-in-Charge at Chhapara Christian Health Centre, has repaid many times over any debt her family owed for her upbringing in the Orphanage. With cheerful hard work, reliability and Christian leadership, she epitomises all that is best in Indian womanhood.

Dr Helen Ramsay came to India from Australia in 1955 and settled in Chhapara. A new missionary's first term is taken up largely with learning – local culture, language and perhaps the ways of a colleague from a different country! By the second term one is able to contribute more. So it was with Helen. Her annual report for 1963 described a highlight of her second term:

"This year has seen some advance in our medical work. You may remember that I took some training in Ophthalmology in the latter half of 1962. I had hoped to begin cataract surgery on my return to Chhapara, but no patients offered themselves. I knew there were many in the villages needing operation so I decided to seek them out. We visited some of the nearer villages, saw patients obviously needing operation but again none was willing for it. After some months of inactivity, I received a letter from Dr Roy Ebenezer, the Indian professor under whom I had studied in Vellore, South India, kindly offering to come for an Eye Camp in August. At rather short notice, his plans were changed and he actually came in September.

"The camp necessitated some planning on our part. Publicity had to be given, so 2,000 handbills were printed and distributed in neighbouring towns and villages. Accommodation for an unknown number of patients had to be provided so the Mission School building was taken over and classes were held in other buildings or in the open. A school room provided a large operating theatre, which was well scrubbed and fitted with two operating tables and all other necessary equipment.

"Dr Roy arrived at 4 p.m. on a Monday and saw a hundred and fifty patients by 9 p.m. At night, after dinner, Miss Dunlop and I continued preparations in theatre until 2 a.m., and were up again at 5 a.m. After a clear Christian testimony given by Dr Roy to the assembled patients and their relatives, more patients were examined. Operating began about 9.30 a.m. and continued until 1.30 a.m. the next morning – forty-four operations being performed on thirty-seven patients.

"The help we received from many was outstanding. Miss Macdonald had left two weeks earlier for Britain. Dr Mackay was in Bombay meeting Miss Macleod. Miss Dunlop and I were the only trained medical staff available. Even Mrs Lall, our nurse, was on maternity leave. From the neighbouring mission in Seoni, Miss McNeel, a nurse, and Dr Jessie McMahon came to watch at 10 a.m., and remained to work hard till 10 p.m. Of her own volition Mrs Lall left her ten-day-old baby to work in theatre all day and till midnight. Our cook, Charan, stayed up to give us dinner at 2 a.m. when operations were finished. Non-Christian businessmen from the village were involved, not only supplying free cooked food for all poor patients but also holding torches for the surgeon while he operated and doing whatever else they could to help. Some of these men stayed on duty till all operations were finished. Students from the local Teachers' Training College were in attendance for ten days and helped in any way necessary, particularly in distributing free food to the seventeen patients who needed it. One of our Christian men who is retired was in voluntary attendance day and night for the ten days.

"On the day of operation the Civil Surgeon from Seoni and his assistant visited us and a few days later the Collector paid us a visit. The townspeople commented freely on Dr Roy's care of his patients and on his Christian attitude.

"Dr Roy examined more patients the next morning and left at mid-day. We did the follow-up work and were glad of Miss Flora Macleod's efficient help on her return from Scotland.

"Not only were the great majority of operations completely successful but Dr Roy achieved one of his stated objects in coming, that of giving our hospital a name for eye work. Since then we have continued to do eye surgery and to treat an increasing number of eye patients. The work is tremendously satisfying. For most of our patients a cataract operation is not just something optional. It means sight and the ability to earn one's daily bread, instead of blindness and abject poverty. To watch a recent patient as she saw the face of her five-year-old son for the first time in three years; to see patients leave hospital walking alone after having been led about for years impresses on us our privilege in being able to help those in desperate need. We find too that these patients, lying quietly in hospital with bandaged eyes, are most receptive to the Gospel message. We pray that some of these may say, as did the blind man whose eyes were opened by Christ, 'Lord, I believe,' and that they may worship Him."

That Eye Camp was indeed a landmark in the care of very needy people. But even in rural India time does not stand still. Fifteen years later, in 1978, Helen reviewed the situation:

"In 1957, after completing language study, I began work in Chhapara. Sister Dunlop had worked there for ten years before that date, and her warm-hearted personality and beautiful Hindi had established an enviable relationship with the people of Chhapara and the surrounding villages. With this basis and her continuing guidance and help, the Dispensary work soon flourished exceedingly. Out-patient numbers increased, sometimes to an unmanageable degree. One had to deal hurriedly with the trivia in order to have time with the really sick. I would feel exhausted after a five-hour session which involved coping with crowds who were naturally impatient after a long wait; dealing with the sick and with their relatives who had to have long explanations given as to why my ideas of treatment differed from theirs; and frequent haggling over money, no matter how small the amount asked.

"I would plod home and nearing the bungalow my heart would sink to see a *chakra* standing in the compound. A *chakra* is the passenger equivalent of the bullock-cart and takes two or three people sitting upright, one behind the other. Indian villagers and some Europeans know how to sit comfortably on these things. To me they always represented gross

discomfort. The appearance of one in the compound meant that I was being called to a village, probably four to six miles away. A twelve mile return trip would mean four hours on the *chakra* plus an hour or two in the village. When there were no village calls, there were home visits to Chhapara, evangelistic visits and the babies in our house to be played with and cared for. With few results from evangelism and with frequent ill-health, I received my main satisfaction from the popularity of our Dispensary and the numbers seen.

"But, even then, I was conscious of the need for preventive medicine. Health education and early treatment would have prevented so much of the ill-health we saw. So we started an ante-natal clinic, one afternoon a week. With constant prodding and the lure of free tablets and powdered milk, a few came regularly. But, due to staff shortages, it stopped after a few months.

"Now that I am back in Chhapara, I see big changes. It is eight years since there has been a missionary doctor resident in Chhapara. There are now three Government doctors and five nurses, and many partially-trained private practitioners. So there is not the same demand on us for curative medicine. Also, the very sick are often willing to travel to Lakhnadon to be admitted to our hospital there.

"Our medical staff is now very conscious of the need for preventive medicine. But this is not something we can impose on people according to our will. They have to be educated to realise their need of it and encouraged to take some part in obtaining it. Both of these are very difficult and time-consuming.

"Thus it was decided that our medical work in Chhapara should now have its main emphasis on Community Health. For this we have some advantages. The greatest is Mrs Lall, who is well known and trusted and who has great enthusiasm and ability in her work. Also, we have a long-standing good relationship with the village people. The Dispensary is now known as the Christian Health Centre. It is open three mornings per week. Of these, Thursday is the Maternal and Child Health clinic and attendance numbers are encouraging. The only patients we now admit are maternity cases and there has been a steady rise in these. We do annual medical examinations in the Mission Primary School and some immunisation has been done. Mrs Lall has given health talks in this and a Government Primary School.

"We are attempting to reach most villages within a six-mile radius, giving more care to a population of five thousand within that area. This has included: health education; immunisation of children; a house-to-house case-finding survey giving us an indication of the prevalence of diseases; maternal and child health; prevention of blindness; tuberculosis prevention and treatment; and the training of village health workers.

"Community Health necessarily involves outside financial support. We hope that in time the villagers will see the value of the work and be willing to contribute to it. Even so, other help will always be needed. The Archbishop of Sydney's Overseas Relief Fund and TEAR Fund have given support.

"As we see the slow or even negative response of the people to the most sympathetic, persistent and culturally-adapted health education, we do not wonder at their slow response to spiritual things. Instead we wonder at our poor recourse to prayer. If God alone can give the increase and if we can reach God through prayer, then our duty is clear. 'Ask of me, and for heritage the heathen I'll make thine.'"

what a contrast!

In 1987, Miss Joan Macdonald – a student nurse and daughter of the Rev. Fergus Macdonald, General Secretary of the National Bible Society of Scotland – wrote of her visit to Lakhnadon:

I was surprised at how small the hospital compound is. Its whitewashed buildings looked much whiter in the slides I saw at home. The wards are small, dark and full of patients and relatives. Many sleep on the verandah. It was quite an experience doing a patient's dressing. There are no curtains; so patients, relatives and whoever was around watched intently. It was strange working with non-disposable instruments.

The approach to nursing here is different from that in Scotland. The nurse's rôle is not patient-oriented but task-oriented. This is due, among other things, to customs; the rôle of relatives; and staff shortages. The relatives provide most of the physical and psychological care – for example, they cook food, give it to the patient, wash, give bed-pans as necessary and comfort him.

The hospital has no facilities to receive blood, store it or give it to patients. The laboratory allows only simple tests on blood and urine to be carried out. It is strange to help in a theatre that is very basic and has no sophisticated respiratory equipment. Consequently nearly all operations are done under local or spinal anaesthesia. I still haven't got used to watching patients walk in and out of theatre!

It is quite a shock when bed-bathing some patients to see how thin and malnourished they are. Many are poor people who own next to nothing. Many suffer from malaria, T.B., malnutrition and chest infections, some of which will kill because treatment is too late or because the patient is too weak. But thousands of villagers receive treatment, recover and return to their very poor and simple life-style.

11

Prevention and Cure at Lakhnadon

The arrival of Dr Willie Urquhart at Lakhnadon in 1926 meant that in 1927 Dr Annie Mackay could take her first furlough – after the Foreign Missions' Committee was persuaded that a first term might be as short as six years! In those days, an Indian term was supposed to last seven. Although her own heart was more in evangelistic work among village women in their homes, she advised the Foreign Missions' Committee in Edinburgh that a hospital in Lakhnadon was necessary for the second doctor's work to be effective.

The Rev. Evan MacKenzie, however, recommended a travelling dispensary first, and, on being invalided home in 1927, he gave advice as to details. Eccles Caravan Company of Birmingham made one to specification; Anchor Line carried it free to Bombay; and from there – unlike the Land Rovers of forty years later – it went by rail. It was used for village visits wherever a car could tow it. Twenty-five years later, the Rev. George Sutherland used its chassis to construct a trailer with higher clearance that could be pulled by car or bullocks on rougher roads.

Fourteen miles north of Lakhnadon is the village of Dhuma. Robert Alexander, a dispenser-catechist who had grown up in the Seoni Orphanage, lived and worked there for three years until his death, probably from typhoid, as a young man in 1932. Willie Urquhart, using the travelling dispensary, enjoyed his weekly visits to Dhuma and other villages. He consulted on the *Toriya* also. But building activities and other administrative duties used up his time and energies to a large degree. He was invalided home in 1930. In Edinburgh he advised the Committee that a male missionary **teacher** would be more useful than a male doctor for India. Neither teacher nor doctor was recruited.

Economic depression was world-wide during the thirties and the effect of financial stringency on Free Church foreign missions was marked. Even a trained teacher, a lady who offered for Chhapara in 1935, was advised "not at present". Offers by some nurses for service in India during the twenties and thirties met with a "no vacancy" response from the Foreign Missions' Committee, for finances were very low. It took a trained nurse, the wife of the Rev. Murray Macleod, to explain convincingly in 1934 how essential were both a hospital and a nurse. Even so, another decade passed before the first nursing recruit arrived. Nan Dunlop's loving service to patients and orphan children was given largely in Chhapara.

Dr Annie Mackay's first furlough had culminated on Wednesday 12th September 1928 in "a rousing missionary rally" at Kingussie, where her father was Free Church minister. As reported in "The Monthly Record", the programme was: 3 p.m. Prayer Meeting; 4 p.m. Children's Address; 5 p.m. Tea at the Manse; and 7 p.m. Evening Meeting. The infectious enthusiasm of the Rev. Angus Mackay can well be imagined!

But it was not until she was leaving Scotland for the third time, in November 1934, that Dr Annie pled for "a hospital, well-equipped; need not be large, even with only five beds". The Free Church young people's magazine "The Instructor", edited then by the Rev. R. A. Finlayson, carried encouragement all through the next year to raise the estimated cost – £1,365. In 1936, for "the second mile", the goal was £40–£50 to buy equipment. Decades later, Free Church children again made special efforts and gave Lakhnadon Hospital an excellent well and audio-visual aids.

In October 1936, Dr Jeannie Grant came from Seoni to cut the ribbon, declaring open a modest medical centre – just what the modest ladies had suggested. Built along the north side of the field bought for the Free Church by Mr McNeel in 1924, these buildings were the nucleus for the extended hospital of later years. Regular clinics were attended by women who appreciated a lady doctor's presence. And many patients benefited from attention in their own homes – at considerable cost to the doctor in terms of time and energy.

With the coming of Mary Ann Macdonald to Lakhnadon in 1951, the popularity of the hospital increased even more. When the Leitches visited in 1954, they found that Dr Annie and Sister Merry (as an Indian friend called her) had moved from the *Toriya* to live at the hospital in order to be nearer in-patients. There were no other trained staff. They shared one room that measured twelve feet by twelve, and that for eating, sitting and sleeping. The "young energetic doctor" (Helen Ramsay), newly arrived in

1955, was asked what she thought of her colleagues' living quarters. "You'd better not hear my comments!" she replied.

George Sutherland was allowed to make a special appeal for funds to convert the 1936 out-patient block into a residence; and a building beside the hospital gate was enlarged for clinics. The helper Tarabai, who had earlier taught the orphan children, came to live in the room that had been theirs. This left three small wards for in-patients. Though theoretically there was room for three, often twelve or more patients, plus relatives, were packed in. And still the work grew.

When Flora Macleod and Anne Urquhart arrived from Scotland in 1962, they were welcomed into attractive homes in Chhapara and in Lakhnadon. Personal gifts of money from individuals and groups of praying friends had been used to buy basic furniture and new curtains. There was no luxury except the luxury of a loving atmosphere, and a great sense of humour.

You would scarcely survive without a sense of humour!

Rats liked Mary's room best. At night they scrabbled in papers; chewed through wood; and ran up, along and down the iron bedsteads and rods that supported a mosquito net. They would not take bait. We didn't keep a cat or dog at Lakhnadon for fear of rabies, and chasing rats with a stick was not easy in a small room!

Snakes are more dangerous. Cobras were common on the *Toriya*. When the Rev. Prakash Kumar and his family lived there, for seven years from 1958, they had no toilet facilities except the jungle. What a hazard for their children! One evening a little snake slipped into our Field Council meeting. It made off towards Mary's room, and we did not find it. When living alone in Chhapara, Nan Dunlop survived being bitten by a poisonous snake.

Ants are less spectacular. But just leave a book lying undisturbed and, a day or a week later, about a tenth of it may have disappeared. White ants devour, without trace, a clean-cut irregularly-shaped chunk of any book, no matter how precious. I have experienced this myself. They do not bite people nor go for your food. Black and red ants do, very industriously. **Bed-bugs** are blood-thirsty; so are **mosquitoes**, some carrying malaria.

And so we could go on. Although living standards have improved over the years, these hazards still exist. Yes, a sense of humour is a **must**.

As an institution, the medical work in the early sixties compared unfavourably with other mission hospitals of similar vintage regarding buildings, equipment and the variety of skilled services offered. This was largely deliberate. Dr Annie and her earlier colleagues considered that a big establishment would divert attention and resources from gospel outreach. However, the demand for their skills grew so much that in 1962, using money available locally, they added an extra room to the out-patient block.

The arrival of new recruits that year and the next seemed to confirm the idea of expansion. After a representative of the Christian Medical Association of India had assessed the situation in 1962, plans were made to increase the scope and efficiency of clinical work. The Foreign Missions' Board was enthusiastic.

In 1966 at Lakhnadon, two new wards were built and the original out-patient department of 1936 was incorporated into the in-patient block, so increasing the number of beds to twenty-four. Quarters for Indian staff were added. The kind English businessmen who had agreed with the Board to take responsibility for building insisted that the missionaries must have a modern bungalow. Small and unpretentious from the outside, it boasted tiled floors throughout, fitted cupboards in the kitchen and even the potential for air-conditioning in one room -- innovations unheard-of in the Lakhnadon of those days, although commonplace by the eighties.

Modern conveniences were not without their disadvantages, however. Businessmen from England were accustomed to a reliable supply of electricity. Lakhnadon's, when it came, was erratic, and the fluctuating voltage ruinous to appliances. The air-conditioner, bought with money a friend at home had originally earmarked for a television set, did not survive a year. Lavish expanses of glass were removed twenty summers later and replaced by small windows. Less easily corrected was the size of bedrooms. Unaware that a family might use the house later (how blind can one be!), we single ladies persuaded the architect to make all three bedrooms of one size. When Dr and Mrs MacDonald came in 1973, they could fit little furniture other than a bed into their room!

Dr Donald's surgical abilities were most welcome in Lakhnadon. But the building extensions of 1966 were no longer adequate. The number of beds was increased to forty simply by reducing the space between them and by using a shelter, built for patients' relatives, to accommodate sufferers from tuberculosis. While encouraged that more than £22,000 was given in response to the appeal in Scotland for Lakhnadon Hospital, Donald MacDonald endured many setbacks while that money was being used. There was a chronic shortage of cement, and contractors gave trouble. But patience was rewarded. On 6th April 1982, Nan Dunlop, while on a visit to India, declared the extension open.

Now Lakhnadon Christian Hospital has the basic requirements of a general hospital – X-ray machine, laboratory, surgical theatre, larger out-patient department and administrative offices. Even so, visitors from the West are still aghast at what they see as miserable clinical facilities. They find diesel jeeps uncomfortable, not realising what a relief it is to have vehicles whose spare parts are available locally. It was almost impossible to maintain British Land Rovers. In 1972, the Board Chairman arrived at Lakhnadon with a clutch plate in his coat pocket. But such visitors were rare!

Another visitor was Alan Yuill, a retired builder from Golspie. He came for three months in 1982 to make improvements to mission property. His work was much appreciated, as was that done some time later by two Australians, John Greensill and David Brock. What Mr Yuill considered miserable was the Indian nurses' accommodation. On returning to Scotland he told his story. He was granted permission by the Foreign Missions' Board to appeal for funds and raised £3,893. This, with a similar amount from the Christoffel Blinden Mission (C.B.M.), a German charitable agency, funded the building of a hostel with good facilities for four single ladies. C.B.M. continues to sponsor medical work, particularly for the treatment and prevention of eye disease. The Indian charity EFICOR (the Evangelical Fellowship of India's Committee on Relief and Development) had given a grant in 1977 for building two houses for senior staff. The doctor and the administrator live there now. Married nurses, junior clerical staff and drivers

Simple conditions at Lakhnadon in 1966.

Arun K. Patras Hospital Administrator

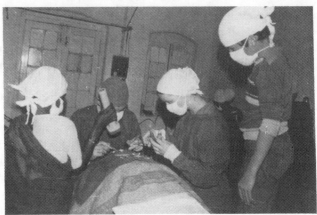

Eye Camp surgery

have quarters that compare fairly well with those in some government hospitals, but still shock Western visitors.

In considering buildings, however, we have moved ahead of developments in organisation.

Part of the tradition passed on from Seoni was that of winter camps for evangelistic outreach in remote parts of the district. The simple medical care offered there was very welcome to villagers in those days when poor transport meant difficulty in reaching hospital. Government nurses had not yet been posted to such places. I have three special memories of camp in the sixties. The first was of a tiger, sighted when we were taking supplies to a camp twenty-five miles out. The second, of tents falling down in a rain storm when we had six toddlers in camp with us. And the third? We had stuck Hindi texts on a mud wall. "Jesus died and rose again," read one lad. There was sheer amazement in his voice as he exclaimed, *"Aray!"*, the equivalent of a vigorous "Wow!" Never before had he even **imagined** that such a thing could happen!

As a follow-on from one such camp, Flora Macleod continued for about a year to hold a weekly clinic, travelling the six miles from Chhapara by bullock-cart. The difference between that type of work and the new-fashioned Community Health (already described by Dr Helen Ramsay) is in the recognition now given to the potential of illiterate villagers, especially women, not only to learn new skills but also to teach them. Suitable persons, selected by popular choice, learn simple health measures. They pass these on to others and so become effective agents for change right there in villages, the strongholds of traditional beliefs.

English doctors in Africa, particularly Maurice King and David Morley, pioneered and publicised this approach in the sixties. So did David Werner in South America. About the same time an Indian doctor-couple, Raj and Mabelle Arole, set up a Comprehensive Rural Health Project at Jamkhed, a village in a famine-stricken area of Maharashtra. This soon became a model for the world, demonstrating not only the wisdom of simplicity but also the unsurpassed ability of Indian Christians to show God's love in action. A little like India's other pilgrims, one after another Free Church Christians, national and expatriate, visited Jamkhed, caught something of the Aroles' vision and brought it back to Madhya Pradesh.

In January 1969, the Land Rover called Nessie (because of Inverness' large share in its cost) took a group of Indian Christians and missionaries from Seoni, Chhapara and Lakhnadon across country eastwards to Orissa, on the shores of the Bay of Bengal. They were delegates to the nineteenth annual conference of the Evangelical Fellowship of India. At that conference, nationals and expatriates, concerned for the future of mission hospitals, took the opportunity to plan together. Sixteen months later, the Emmanuel Hospital Association (E.H.A.), free from the stigma of foreign domination, was registered with the Indian government. In 1974 the Free Church's medical work in both Chhapara and Lakhnadon was incorporated into E.H.A. Mr Lalchuangliana, a Presbyterian from India's north-eastern state of Mizoram, is the Executive Secretary of E.H.A. In 1987, he explained in some detail the development of this organisation:

"Evangelism was the foremost task of mission agencies. However, people under bondage of poverty, sickness and social evils were encountered. In order to alleviate the physical suffering of people and to express the compassion of the Lord Jesus, mission agencies set up hospitals, dispensaries and clinics, thus becoming the forerunners of health services in many less-developed countries. In India about one thousand such health institutions run by Christian missions were in operation when the country became independent in 1947. However, a decline in Christian medical work began to set in in the sixties, when the number of missionary personnel decreased due to various factors, including official restrictions on the entry of new missionaries. The result was that, in terms of institutional services, the number of mission hospitals has become less than half of what it used to be. At the same time, with an expanding population, the need for health and medical services increased drastically.

"Concerned with the decreasing volume of Christian medical services and the prospect of closure of many more hospitals, several key people with evangelical convictions met together, and a vision was granted for the working together of different mission hospitals under one organisation. Thus the Emmanuel Hospital Association was born towards the end of the sixties. The E.H.A.'s official birthday was 18th May 1970, when it was registered and assumed a legal identity.

"The main purpose of E.H.A. is to maintain Christian health and medical services in the name and spirit of the Lord Jesus as an expression of his compassion for the sick and poor regardless of their background. E.H.A. did not come into being merely for the sake of medical services. E.H.A. is concerned with the lost state of the unredeemed and it is seeking to bring people to the Lord Jesus for salvation. However, medical services are not seen as tools or vehicles of evangelism but as worthy expressions of our Christian love and concern in the manner of our Lord Jesus himself.

"In professional matters E.H.A. is convinced of the wisdom of holistic health care and primary health care for the community. As such, community health programmes in villages form a major part of the activities of E.H.A., as well as curative base-hospitals.

"Within a period of five years, E.H.A. consolidated itself and, following extensive consultations, mutual relationships with mission agencies and different hospitals were established. E.H.A. came to be an epitome of mission cooperative enterprise. Completely unrelated mission agencies such as the Mennonite Missions in the U.S.A., the Bible Churchmen's Missionary Society, the Regions Beyond Missionary Union, the Free Church of Scotland Foreign Missions' Board, the International Christian Fellowship, the Presbyterian Church of the U.S.A. and others joined for a common ministry in the Emmanuel Hospital Association.

"Sixteen E.H.A. hospitals, with 1,182 beds and forty doctors, looked after 319,795 patients in a hospital situation during 1986, at an average cost of £3.50 per patient. This amount covers also the surgical services for 10,651 patients, the hospital and nursing care of 32,341 patients and the training of sixty nursing students. Moreover, the lives of hundreds of people in villages are being touched daily through the activities of the community health programmes. That God has owned the ministry of E.H.A. is evident from the fact that so much was done in his name with so little. To God be all the glory and praise.

"Nearly 25% of the financial requirements for the ministry of E.H.A. was met in 1986 by the assistance of God's people outside India. The greatest need in E.H.A. was, is today and will remain committed workers **called** by the Lord to serve in his name. There are more Christian doctors in India than ever before, but the Christian hospitals, despite their dwindling numbers, are constantly short of doctors. We have to pray fervently to the Lord of the harvest to send out workers willing to take the rôle of servants in his name."

In 1988 the withdrawal, for personal and family reasons, of the MacDonald family and Barbara Stone means that there are no Free Church missionaries left in our Indian field at the time of writing. Current government regulations prevent new replacements entering the country from abroad. Indian Christians are taking their place.

Mr. Lalchuangliana (right), Executive Secretary of E.H.A. with Professor A.C. Boyd, Secretary to F.M.B. at the Free Church School in Theology, Larbert, 1985.

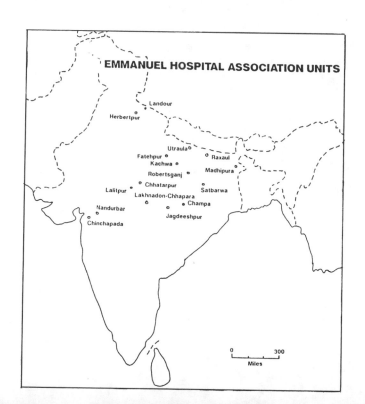

an eight-hour shift

Elizabeth Ferrier wrote of a typical day's work at Lakhnadon Christian Hospital in 1985:

5 a.m: Rise, wash and dress in white uniform sari.

5.45: Walk down from the Toriya *to the hospital. This ten-minute walk is "my" time, when I usually talk to God about my family at home and admire the beauty of the countryside.*

5.55: Enter hospital – Namaste *all round. ("Namaste" is a Hindi greeting used at any time of the day or night.)*

6 a.m: Sit down for report with night nurse. Mixture of Hindi and English.

6.15: Go to theatre to set up trays for operating list. Off with outdoor shoes; on with theatre sandals and mask. Set out trays using sterilised Cheatles forceps to lift out instruments, a skill not easily acquired. It takes time to learn not to drop anything nor let the Cheatles accidentally brush a drape.

6.40 or whatever: Start the round of morning injections: could be five, or thirty. A painful round; none-too-sharp needles, boiled and reboiled till all sharpness is gone.

7 a.m: Ward prayers. Everyone who can packs into the Female Ward and a Christian man from the staff leads. We sing, have a reading from the Bible, a short exposition and prayer.

7.15: Staff prayers in hospital prayer-room. All Christian staff come together for this. We pray for our work and that of other E.H.A. hospitals.

7.30: Theatre. Might be one, might be seven operations; very varied list.

10 a.m: After theatre, a welcome coffee break. Depending on work, could be twenty-five, twenty, fifteen minutes or less.

10.30: Ward round. Doctor, sister, nurse and auxiliary all go round to discuss progress and management of patients.

11 a.m: Medicine round. At some time during the morning, you have found time to put out all the medicines for from twelve to fifty people. No drug-trolley. Each person's tablets are put in a little pot, with the name of the patient on a piece of paper. This could be a difficult twenty minutes, especially for the expatriate nurse! All the Pyarilall's, Ramabai's, Tulsa's etc. can be confusing – even uproarious.

11.30 or thereabouts: Set to on the dressings. These again could be many and varied – burns, leg ulcers, abscesses, amputations, etc. This could take quite a

time. And soon it's.....
   2 p.m: The next nurse comes on duty and you hand over to her.

   A very broad outline. As well as this "routine" there are the juchki-bai's *(maternity cases), who wait for no-one. They are the real thrill. They can take time. There are intravenous infusions to be checked, bottles to be changed, and post-natal checks. Often there are very ill patients who should be in Intensive Care – tetanus cases, eclamptics (no "pre-" about it!), diabetics, snake-bite victims, and the major post-op cases; hourly aspirations of fluid from the stomach via naso-gastric tube; the giving of* OMNOPON; *bed-bathing; the comforting of anxious patients and relatives; plus many other varied occurrences in any one day.*
   Eight hours may not seem a long time; but a more demanding, stressful, exciting, exhilarating and stimulating shift I have never experienced.

View from the Toriya. Lakhnadon Town is in background (left) and hospital in right middleground.

IV AN INDIAN CHURCH

'Christ loved the church and gave himself up for her.' [Eph. 5.25]

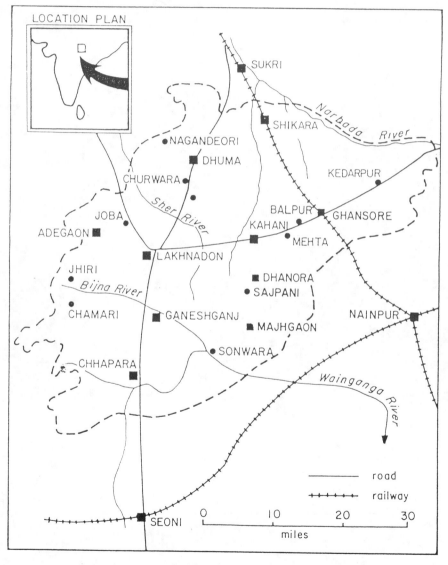

Lakhnadon tehsil

12
Mainly the Mission

Lakhnadon Church

How did the Free Church of Central India develop?

We think of two families first, because their homes are some of the few in the **Lakhnadon** area, outwith mission property, where the name of Christ has been honoured over many years.

From the earliest days of the Free Church in Lakhnadon, the Salve family has been part of the Christian witness there. Of Methodist background and from another part of Madhya Pradesh, Mr Salve (senior) was a government employee when Evan and Eva Mackenzie arrived in 1924. He helped them find temporary accommodation and later arranged for the purchase of the "cottage and garden" site where the church now stands, not far from the main bazaar.

The Salves' own property is also fairly central in Lakhnadon, near enough to the bus-stand to allow you to wait there before travelling. Mr Salve's son, physically active most of his life in spite of having suffered a stroke in his youth, rented for many years the twelve acres of agricultural land beside the hospital. He died in 1988. His wife Ruthbai was a faithful helper at the hospital in Dr Annie Mackay's day. Their marriage was remembered as one where the vows seemed unusual. Dr Willie Urquhart's Lochalsh accent confused the Hindi sounds "ch" and "j", so that instead of **joining** them in marriage, he seemed to encourage them to **leave** each other! However, the marriage lasted intact for fifty years. Of their six daughters, the eldest is married in New York and another in London. A third, Lata, married Yunas Lall, a brother of Mrs Taramoni Lall of Chhapara. Lata teaches in the government Girls' High School at Lakhnadon and is a loyal member of the Free Church. Other Christian families in government service have lived in Lakhnadon town for some years at a time. Only the Salve household has maintained a constant Christian presence in the town centre since the 1920s.

Mr Laxman Forbes (1889-1963) was employed as an evangelist from 1924. He acquired a small-holding adjacent to the Mission Hospital. His son-in-law, Mr Kothare, now a widower, still lives there, alone. Belonging to a Pentecostal group in Jabalpur, he has been critical at times of our practices but is now content to attend the Free Church in Lakhnadon when not visiting his children elsewhere. Whether or not one of the Kothare children will yet return to bring up a family in the old home remains to be seen. Employment is not easily found in this rural setting. During the 1950s and 1960s the children were part of the Sunday School at Lakhnadon.

Before 1935, worship services were held at the Salves' home and on the *Toriya*. The complex of buildings on the hill so impressed local people then that they called it *Padre-ganj* (*"ganj"* meaning village). In 1935 Murray Macleod, using a legacy of £40 10s, had a brick church built in Lakhnadon town. On 15th August 1948, the first anniversary of Independence Day, a group of Hindu government officials attended the service there. That was a rare occurrence. Although the door is always open during worship time, it was and is unusual for people of a non-Christian background to come in. The vestry has been used at times as a clinic, and during the 1960s as a Reading Room. Hindu and Muslim children have attended Sunday School there, at the hospital and on the *Toriya*. Of course, old greetings cards with bright pictures are the big attraction. If challenged on their way to Sunday School they would say they were going for a "photo"! Even so, the seed of the Word has germinated in some hearts.

Because the majority of people attending the means of grace at Lakhnadon are employed at the hospital, Sunday evening services and mid-week meetings have sometimes been held in homes nearer the hospital. Since a cinema was built beside the church in the early 1980s, serious thought has been given to re-siting the church, because noise and litter could be problems. But no move has yet been made.

During the first five years of the Free Church Mission's presence in **Chhapara**, services on the Lord's Day were usually held on the verandah of a private home or in the small school building. If no man was ready to lead, Elizabeth Macleod conducted what amounted to family worship.

After the opening of the new school premises in 1930, services were held there regularly until 1963. The Elizabeth Macleod Memorial Reading Room was then built in response to the presence in Chhapara of students attending the government Teachers' Training College. That College functioned from 1960 until 1979. Nan Dunlop, on home leave in 1962, was so persuasive in encouraging people to give money for the Reading Room that it was whispered she should be detained in Scotland to work on behalf of the Sustentation Fund! The Reading Room fund grew, and grew. Helen Ramsay, responsible for building plans in Chhapara, had to be advised by the Board Secretary that her estimated cost was much too low.

The Reading Room, opened on 11th February 1964, stands on a prominent corner of the plot between Mission School and bungalow at Chhapara. Since so much money had been given, another building of similar size was built adjoining it, to be used as a church. Seating about fifty, it has housed the congregation at Chhapara until now. Yet it has never been reckoned to be "a proper church". Nan Dunlop, revisiting India, cut the first turf in the vacant part of that same plot of land on 2nd February 1989, for the erection of a new church building. The local Christians aim to raise one third of its cost. Inflation, however, is running high. The Foreign Missions' Board in Scotland is contributing some money. Friends in Australia are helping too – and not only with cash, but also with the building skills of John Greensill, who is no stranger in Chhapara.

During this century, many other Indian men as well as Mr Forbes have been employed in church work. The Secession Mission had acquired small houses in outlying villages and passed three on to the Free Church in 1924. Before they were sold in 1969, one evangelist was usually settled in **Ghansore** and another in **Kahani** – twenty-one and thirteen miles east of Lakhnadon respectively.

At **Dhuma**, fourteen miles north on the Jabalpur road, Mr Godwin Laxman spent most of his thirty-six years' service. Son of an elder in Seoni, he had received informal training there as evangelist and dispenser. His grandmother was Radhabai, the Biblewoman who had been Elizabeth Macleod's constant companion when visiting homes in and around Seoni. Of cheerful disposition, he became well-accepted in Dhuma as a medical practitioner. He shared preaching duties with his colleagues, especially at Lakhnadon. His family members sometimes attended church with him and sometimes a meeting was held in their home. Before retiring in 1969, Godwin bought the small property belonging to the Mission in Dhuma. Now a widower, he lives elsewhere with family members, some of whom hold senior posts in other Christian hospitals. His youngest son, whose interest in politics is keen, lives on in Dhuma. Whatever the unseen influence of Christian witness there since an evangelist was first sent in 1915, there is little vital evidence of it today, nor in Ghansore, nor in Kahani.

Between Ghansore and Kahani is a Roman Catholic mission station, staffed by a priest and nuns from South India. They have schools in several villages and run a dispensary, from which they refer patients to Lakhnadon Christian Hospital. That work was begun in the early 1940s as

an offshoot from a Dutch Roman Catholic mission to the east, across the
Narmada River. Considerable interest in the gospel had been shown by
people in that area during the time of winter camps, organised by Murray
Macleod. He laboured intensively, cycling many arduous miles. He even
bought a small house where he and his family lived for a time. Then a keen
Indian Christian whom he knew from Language School stayed there for
about two years. Groups of Hindu villagers used to attend Christian worship
services there. Free Church people in Scotland prayed for individuals by
name. And there was a burden for families. Lena Gillies wrote in 1942,
"We aim at interesting groups in the hope that whole villages will abandon
their idols". The Macleods went on home-leave at the end of 1945. When
they returned in 1947 it was for less than two years. Not until 1951 was
the next ordained recruit, the Rev. George Sutherland, ready to minister in
Hindi. And so that most promising patch was ceded, unwittingly, to the
Roman Catholics.

It is difficult to assess now whether the Free Church could or should
have retained Murray Macleod in her ranks. The 1944 General Assembly
was advised by Elizabeth Macleod that it would be "nothing short of a
calamity" if this "truly evangelical preacher" were to leave. His reservations
about and later his rejection of infant baptism were the obvious reason for
his resignation. Ill-health in his family, inadequate financial provision to
cover this, and the Committee's refusal to allow him wider scope were
additional factors. Unusually fluent in Hindi and gifted in Biblical exposition,
he was burdened to contribute more to Indian Christian literature and to
have a part in theological education in India.

His gifts were not wasted during his time in the Free Church. Special
services, at New Year time particularly, were blessed to the orphan children.
During the rainy season each year (mid-June to mid-October), when floods
and mud hindered access to villages, the evangelists came together and he
taught them Old Testament, New Testament, Systematic Theology (based
on the Shorter Catechism), elementary Church History, Homiletics and
Apologetics with special reference to Hinduism and Islam. During home-
leave too his preaching was of lasting benefit, especially in the congregations
of Partick and the Free North.

One of the men attending those classes at Lakhnadon was the Rev.
Samuel Washington (1893-1964). Ordained in the Methodist Church, he
worked in the Free Church Mission from 1940 until he retired. Up to
1959 he was the only Indian, apart from visitors, to administer the
sacraments in the Free Church area.

Of the twenty-five persons at the Lord's Table at Lakhnadon in 1952,
the majority were mission workers who had grown up in Christian families
or the Orphanage. But throughout the decades there have been individuals,

here and there, coming to faith in Christ from a Hindu background. In 1934, a middle-aged Gondh lady was left at Lakhnadon with the missionaries. Her name, Basanti-bai, means "springtime". Because her sores had become infested with maggots she was regarded as an outcast. Responding to the offer of the gospel, she became a bright Christian. She was baptised and received into church membership. Her physical condition improved. In later years she lived contentedly, with a cat, in a tiny room at the Chhapara Dispensary, acting as watchman. Illiterate all her days, she learned much by listening to the Biblewomen and was happy when she herself was telling of God's love. She died in 1955.

More prestigious by worldly standards was Munshiram Tiwari (1894-?1970). A Brahman priest, he too came first to the missionaries because of physical pain. By God's grace, through reading the Bible, prayer and conversation with Murray Macleod he came to faith in Christ. In 1945, after deliberating for two years, he transferred with his immediate family from Lakhnadon town to the *Toriya*. He moved by night, to avoid interference from other family members. The mother of his children, who was not a Brahman, also believed. They were joined in Christian marriage and baptised. At that time Tiwari vowed that he would never again set foot in his home town of Lakhnadon unless he reverted to Hinduism, which he never did. He was soon appointed to the mission staff as evangelist and part-time teacher in Chhapara School. In 1949 he was elected vice-president of Chhapara Municipal Council. After serving in Kahani for some years, he moved to the *Toriya,* where he lived in the Little Bungalow until retiring in 1966. His latter years were spent with a married son in Maharashtra.

Murray Macleod's leaving Lakhnadon in 1949 was a blow to Tiwari. George Sutherland, arriving in India in 1950, found it difficult to understand him, as did later missionaries. With Nan Dunlop, whose grasp of Hindi was exceptionally good, Tiwari had better rapport.

He welcomed former friends and relatives who came to reason with him, explaining his hope in Christ from God's Word. On visits to outlying villages, his former status as a Brahman priest was sometimes recognised and he was not averse to a good meal, given as a token of respect! In 1955 Duncan Leitch reported after his stay in Lakhnadon:

"Mr Tiwari is, in my opinion, the ablest of our evangelists. He is a strong, forceful character; as preacher and organiser he has gifts above the average. I believe him to be a truly born-again man who, in the face of many difficulties and not a little opposition, has been faithful to the Lord, for whom he has a deep love. It is to be regretted that, because of a vow he took at his conversion, he feels prohibited from entering Lakhnadon and therefore cannot attend services in the church nor undertake the work of an evangelist in the town where he might be more useful than any of his colleagues."

With hindsight, it is easy to say that to employ such a recent convert as an evangelist was unwise. The Free Church magazine "From the Frontiers" quoted from John M. L. Young's address to a Reformed Ecumenical Synod meeting in 1969: "Missionaries have often been tempted, in the interests of speeding evangelism, to take a promising young convert and pay him to evangelise. Dependency fails to feed the spirit of responsibility, often leaving the **impression that the responsibility for the church's affairs belongs to the one who is paying the bills.** A foreign-paid worker promotes the idea in the community that Christianity is a foreign religion impossible of natural growth or acceptance in their land. Where nationalism is strong the worker may bring the contempt of the community on himself and the church for being 'bought' to desert the local religion for a foreign one" (my emphasis).

Tiwari had, by turning to Christ, lost his old employment. He had a family to support. His abilities as thinker and speaker were considerable. If he had been able more obviously to integrate his new faith with local culture, in so far as that culture was compatible with God's Word, more secret believers might have been encouraged to come into the open. (Compatibility with God's Word is of course not necessarily the same as compatibility with Scottish culture.) In conversation with Tiwari, one sensed undeveloped potential. He loved the Lord but lacked nurture in Christian fellowship and teaching. As with other aspects of the church's life in India, only the day of judgment will make known the fruit of his witness.

In the early 1950s, Mr McNeel of Seoni sent Mr Panna Lall on loan to Chhapara. He was a young man who had grown up in the Secession Orphanage and had trained as an evangelist at the Canadian Presbyterian Bible School at Jhansi, Madhya Pradesh. Although invited back to Seoni, he settled in Chhapara, marrying Taramoni Lall there in 1959. Each has now completed more than thirty years' service.

For many years he helped with registration of patients at the Dispensary, as well as telling of Christ. Mr Lall suffers from asthma and is not as active now in village evangelism as formerly. He continues to teach Bible at Chhapara Mission School. After buying the small house which they used to rent from the mission, the Lalls set about enlarging and improving it. Listening to their plans for this some years ago, I was interested in the main reason given. Their children were coming to the age when marriage must be arranged and it was considered important that prospective in-laws be favourably impressed. This concern for material good is matched by attention to the young people's spiritual welfare.

There were high hopes in 1958 that a final-year student at the Free Church College, Archie Boyd, and his fiancée Doreen Paterson would go to India as long-term missionaries. They married; a passage to Bombay was booked and their Farewell arranged. Then a second medical opinion said "No". And "No" it remained. He entered the ministry in Scotland instead.

The Boyds' interest in India did not wane. Subodh Sahu, a prominent Indian Christian who had visited Lakhnadon, stayed with them at Shettleston in 1969. Impressed by Mr Boyd's preaching, he invited him to lecture at the 1971 Congress on Evangelism in his home state of Orissa. After a refreshing time at the Congress, Mr Boyd made his way to the Free Church area. Chhapara, first seen in the quiet of a moonlit night and "for so long the destination of one's dreams", seemed dearly familiar to him. Appointed as part-time Secretary to the Foreign Missions' Board in 1979, he has had reason to return to India on several occasions and is a welcome visitor each time.

Apart from the Boyds themselves, probably no one was more disappointed at the cancellation of plans in 1958 than George Sutherland, who saw it as "almost a catastrophe". He resigned from service in India the following year. There was encouragement, however, in another person. Mr Leitch's 1955 Report contained this additional note: "Prakash, one of our own orphans, is taking an evangelist's course at Allahabad and should be ready for service in the Mission in the summer of 1957. He promises well." In October 1959 at Lakhnadon, a few days before leaving India, the Rev. George Sutherland, in the company of ministers and elders from Seoni, conducted the service of ordination and induction of the Rev. Prakash Kumar. This was done with the express permission of the General Assembly in Edinburgh.

To find himself so soon the only minister in the Indian field of the Free Church of Scotland must have been quite daunting for a young man. An unassuming person, Prakash Kumar has not found his leadership rôle easy. His wife Premlata, brought up in an orphanage of the Regions Beyond Missionary Union in North Bihar and trained in Allahabad as a Biblewoman, has been and is a great support to him. For the first six years of his ministry and of their marriage, they lived on the *Toriya* at Lakhnadon. The part of the Big Bungalow where they stayed had no running water nor indoor toilet. It was far from the bazaar, which meant they carried their heavy shopping a long way. Salaries were small. During those days they repaid five hundred rupees of their wedding expenses. That amounted to over 90% of the total cost of about £35. In later years, the marriage expenses of younger orphans were met largely by money gifted by supporting congregations and individuals.

Prakash Kumar and his wife welcomed the move to Chhapara in 1965. There his position as minister remained the same. In addition, he took on responsibility for the Reading Room, built in 1963. This was convenient for him as he studied privately for and secured his B.A. degree. There had been delay in opening the Reading Room for lack of suitable staff. Abraham Shastri from Kerala had resigned after manning it for a year. During its first fifteen years, the Reading Room attracted many trainee teachers from Chhapara's Government College, which closed in 1979. It is a convenient place for informal discussion. Millions of homes in the cities, towns and villages of India have a radio. Christian broadcasts – by Far East Broadcasting Association, Back to the Bible, Trans-World Radio, to name a few agencies – are popular. Correspondence Courses are advertised by radio and thousands enrol. Some men come to the Chhapara Reading Room to talk over these courses with Prakash. The stock of books kept is very poor. There is next to no demand for English and the range of Christian books in Hindi is limited. The Bible, however, is always available.

Added responsibility came to the Rev. Prakash Kumar and his wife three months after their move from Lakhnadon, when *Bari Mama* retired as Matron of the Orphanage. From a tiny house by the School, they came with their family to live in equally cramped accommodation behind the missionaries' bungalow. They endured that for four years, until the new Orphanage was built in 1969. It was home to the extended family for eleven years, before being taken over for use as a Health Centre. By 1980 Prakash had had his own house built. Fairly substantial by local standards, it gives good scope for hospitality.

In spite of having grown up with most of the senior members of the church in Chhapara, Prakash Kumar retains their respect and confidence. He has earned that of the younger members also. Under God, he is responsible for much of the cohesion of the Christian community there now.

Mr. Panna Lall and his wife Taramoni.

Rev. Prakash Kumar and his wife Premlata.

Artist's impression of a quiet morning at Chhapara. Reading Room on left; Mission Bungalow on right.

life and death

Nan Dunlop told of three days' work at Chhapara in the early fifties:

One hot afternoon just after lunch we heard someone call, "Miss Sahib, Miss Sahib!" in very urgent tones. Two women from a village three miles away stood at the door requesting that we accompany them to a confinement case. The road lay through jungle and through fields of hemp well above head height. We went on foot.

On arrival, we found the patient, a girl of less than fifteen, seriously ill with high fever, lying on a heap of rags in a corner on the mud floor. Can you picture the poor thing lying there, getting no sympathy from her hard-hearted old mother-in-law, who thought of nothing except the trouble the girl's illness was causing? After treatment with penicillin the girl's condition improved slightly, but we still felt it necessary to remain with her overnight.

At dusk, after great consultation with the men who had returned from their work in the fields, a woman brought two wadded quilts, one of which we used as a mattress and the other as a cover. She also asked what we would eat. I agreed to bread and milk as offered, but there was much consternation when Miss Macdonald said she would have tea, for no-one seemed to have any tea. However, enough was got from the patail – the headman of the village – to make two cups. We wanted the tea made with water only and not as they make it – with milk, sugar, salt, ginger and what not. They decided to light a fire of dried cow-dung outside and made the tea while we sat nearby on a wooden bed-frame. Finally we got our fried unleavened bread, sugar and tea. The moon had risen and many people gathered to watch us eat. This gave us an opportunity to sing and speak for the Master after the meal was over. They listened for a long time and then asked that we sing again.

We were very tired indeed when we lay down on a bed which certainly was never made for two. Even with the cows and goats tethered around us, we might have slept if it had not been for the bugs.

The following morning the patient was well enough for us to leave her. We went home and had breakfast and a welcome wash, returning in a few hours to stay with her that day and night. During this time we had further opportunity for witness. Saturday morning saw such marked improvement in her general condition that we felt we could leave her until we were sent for.

We didn't get our much-looked-for night in a clean, comfortable bed, for, just as we lay down, there was another maternity call. The husband who came to call us – big, strong, healthy fellow that he was – said he was a beggar and couldn't pay any fee. However, we went to see the patient, who would have needed a doctor. But as we had no means of getting word to Dr Annie Mackay, we got to work ourselves. We were very glad when the patient didn't die, as we had no experience of such a case and were working according to a treatment book. We got home at 2:30 a.m., very happy and grateful to God. At 5 a.m. the people from the other village came to call us again. We were tired but enjoyed the walk through the fields in the early morning light. The life of this patient also was spared. But neither of the babies was alive.

Will you pray for the people of that village – Daori? They welcome us when we go to speak to them and have asked us to come often.

A Hindu Sadhu *('holy man')*

13
The Free Church of Central India

*The Minister and 'The Men' 1965, Rev. Prakash Kumar, Abraham Shastri,
Godwin Laxman, Munshiran Tiwari, Peter MacLeod and Pana Lall..*

What about the **congregation** of which the Rev. Prakash Kumar became
the minister in 1959?

It had been constituted in 1956 by resolution of the General Assembly
in Edinburgh. The relevant part of the 1955 finding reads:

"The General Assembly resolve that all persons in their Indian
Mission adhering to the doctrine and worship of the Free Church
of Scotland shall form the Free Church Congregation of
Lakhnadon and Chhapara. The General Assembly instruct Rev.
George Sutherland, whom they recognise as Minister of the
Charge, to prepare a Communion Roll comprising the names of
those admitted to Sealing Ordinances dispensed in the Mission,
and that those inserted in the Communion Roll be regarded as
Communicants in the Free Church of Scotland congregation of
Lakhnadon and Chhapara. In the absence of a Kirk Session they
direct Mr Sutherland on his return to India to call a meeting of
the Congregation for the purpose of electing elders and, when
these shall have been duly elected according to the Practice of the
Free Church of Scotland, they further direct him to ordain and
induct them to office. They, together with their Minister, shall be
recognised as the Kirk Session of the Congregation."

149

During the thirty years before 1956, church matters had been properly conducted, but without an ecclesiastical structure. Now there was one congregation, with its Kirk Session: that of Lakhnadon and Chhapara. But thirty more years were to pass before a Presbytery would emerge.

Coming to India five years after the ordination of the Rev. Prakash Kumar, the Rev. Ian McKenzie took time to settle down, get married and learn enough Hindi for preaching. You can make do with far less language in medical practice! Then he worked with the Kirk Session to increase understanding of Reformed truth. The Field Council, however, remained the place where most decisions were taken, and only one Indian member of Kirk Session, the Rev. Prakash Kumar, sat on it.

All through the 1960s and into the 1970s it was taken for granted by the missionaries (or at least by the ladies, who were in the majority) that they were responsible for decision making – maintenance of buildings, including the churches; who would be invited for special meetings; where camp might be held; the appointment of an evangelist at Lakhnadon. Perhaps finance had something to do with this state of affairs. There was need for the warning already quoted from Young, that financial dependency may create the "impression that the responsibility for the church's affairs belongs to the one who is paying the bills". Transfer of responsibility to Indian shoulders did not come easily. The maternal instinct of lady missionaries tended to perpetuate a dependent attitude among the orphans, even after they had grown up. There was a chronic shortage of ordained men who would give priority to church development. Although the Chhapara School had an Indian headmaster from its early days, most senior people in medical work were foreigners. In Lakhnadon particularly, organisation of and local financial support for church affairs depended largely on them. But during the seventies there was gradual change.

Ian McKenzie's aim in moving to Jabalpur was to plant a church that would be independent of institutional work and away from a mission compound. The choice of accommodation in Jabalpur – a very ordinary little house in a lower middle-class suburb – helped the McKenzies to identify with their neighbours. In this last quarter of the twentieth century, India's middle class is growing fast in villages and towns, as well as in cities. But at that point in time, 1976, some of us Westerners almost envied the McKenzies their close, though costly, identification with the local people. Shortage of space meant that Ian had no place he could call his own as a study. Concerned that the orphan children should not feel different from their peers, Alina often spent hours mending their clothes, rather than buying new ones. When any of the children needed hospital treatment, as some did at Vellore in South India because of chronic ear disease, she was Mother to the extent of being admitted too, to do all that a close relative normally does. Sometimes another missionary or Indian colleague also helped out. And all was taken for granted by the children.

Francis Masih of Rajasthan (West India), a young graduate of the Reformed Presbyterian Seminary – then at Roorkee, now at Dehra Dun, U.P. – joined the McKenzies as house-father to the five orphan boys who were attending High School in Jabalpur. Two years later, in 1978, his marriage was arranged to a Nagpur girl, Rekha, a member of the Operation Mobilisation team that had been visiting Premnagar. Francis and Rekha left in 1980 and joined the Church of North India. In 1982 they returned, to work in Lakhnadon, where he was ordained to the ministry in February 1984. Six months later their request for transfer to Jabalpur was granted. Again dissatisfied, they returned to Lakhnadon, but early in 1989 he resigned from the Free Church. It appears that they want to work independently of the Free Church and are arranging their own support.

The lack of a steady resident ministry at Lakhnadon over the last twenty years has been harmful. The Rev. Prakash Kumar left for Chhapara in 1965, and the Rev. Ian McKenzie in 1967. Since then there has been a succession of evangelists. Some, such as Abraham Shastri, have been first-class. Recruited first for Chhapara Reading Room, he later served in Lakhnadon from 1965 to 1969. Unlike some from Kerala, he learned Hindi well. One forthright sermon from Daniel chapter 3 verse 18, **"But if not"** (the Hindi version also has three short words) stays in my mind even today. His wife Mary, an excellent staff-nurse also from Kerala, was one person who helped Heather Beaton and me to survive through the traumatic days of 1966, when the hospital at Lakhnadon was being altered and extended around our ears – and still patients crowded in! I am not sure why the Shastris left. To my shame be it said, I was too busy then to listen to people. They may now be in the Middle East, or farther west.

Other men have done the work of an evangelist at Lakhnadon for a few months or years. It is not an easy place. Tiwari's profession of faith in Christ is remembered and possibly resented. The medical work tends to overshadow other Christian activities. It is probably true that over the years more people have heard the gospel through this avenue (the medical work) than through any other connected with our witness. There may be many secret believers among them. But secret believers lack teaching and are lost to the visible church. Although the staff recruited by the Emmanuel Hospital Association join in worship and fellowship, most have not developed a deep loyalty to the local church. Those who grew up in our own Orphanage feel more at home in Chhapara. The area cries out for a shepherd prepared to give a lead in loving service for Jesus' sake. Towards the end of 1989, the Rev. Yohan Das was appointed evangelist at Lakhnadon.

In 1979 the Rev. David John joined the Jabalpur team. While still an orphanage schoolboy in Seoni, he was converted under Cyril Thomson's preaching. His wife has a similar background. After teaching for thirteen years in the Seoni Mission High School, David John studied at Union Bible Seminary in Maharashtra. If the Church of North India's local Bishop had had his way, training would have been at a more liberal college. But the Rev. Robert McMahon and his wife Dr Jessie, Church of Scotland missionaries at Seoni, helped him have his four-year B.D. course at an evangelical establishment. Ordained in the Church of North India, he was appointed to the city charge of Raipur in Madhya Pradesh. But he found the episcopal form of church government distasteful, and the pay was inadequate for the needs of his growing family.

The Premnagar congregation began with Christian people whose own churches were so far away in Jabalpur city centre that they were out of touch. A church with adjoining manse was built in 1979. The witness extended to another suburb, Vijainagar, about two miles distant. Property acquired there in 1984 was altered to provide church and manse. David John ministered at Vijainagar from 1979. In 1983 he moved to Premnagar to replace Ian McKenzie. Mr S. K. Lall, a brother-in-law of Mr Alexander, the headmaster at Chhapara Mission School, was appointed evangelist at Vijainagar in 1988.

In 1980 the Mission Superintendent, Ian McKenzie, had gone to Scotland to consult with the Foreign Missions' Board. Discussion was long and prayerful. Was it or was it not feasible to continue a commitment to work in India? Already visas for several expatriates willing to serve there had been refused. It was likely that for family or personal reasons the missionaries currently serving would leave within the next decade. The medical work had been incorporated into the Emmanuel Hospital Association in 1974. The School would become self-governing. And the Orphanage had only two teenage children left. The Reformed Presbyterian Church in Uttar Pradesh (U.P.), several hundred miles to the north, has a doctrinal basis that we could accept. Would it be wiser to encourage our Christian people in the Free Church area to merge with some other body?

It was decided that the Reformed Presbyterians in U.P. were too far away in physical terms and that nearer churches were too far removed doctrinally. Mr McKenzie returned to India to form a Church Development Committee, with the express aim of seeing a truly national church emerge.

When the McKenzies' service in India was complete in 1984, Dr MacDonald became Mission Administrator (not Superintendent), a term used to show the changing rôle of the expatriate. He was able, with help from Indian colleagues, to draw up three necessary documents for the emerging Free Church of Central India (F.C.C.I.) – the name chosen by

Rev. David John and his wife at Premnagar Free Church.

David Brock, Vinodh Das, John Greensill and William Chalate (driver).

the local Christians. They were: a Constitution, to give legal standing; a Policy of Employment, laying down terms and conditions of service for F.C.C.I. workers; and a book on procedure, adapted from "The Practice of the Free Church of Scotland". He also produced material for the ministers to use in preparing men for ordination as elders.

Elders were elected and ordained in Chhapara and Jabalpur during 1985. Donald MacDonald served as Lakhnadon's elder. Chhapara and Lakhnadon separated to form individual congregations, each with a Kirk Session. In Jabalpur, Premnagar and Vijainagar were separate congregations under one Kirk Session. This led to the inauguration of the Presbytery of the Free Church of Central India at Lakhnadon on 20th September 1986. Professor Archie Boyd represented the home church on that occasion.

Professor Boyd was also the first of a special kind of visitor. The Foreign Missions' Board resolved that, since ordained missionaries can no longer settle in India, they will send a minister for six to eight weeks every second year to encourage the F.C.C.I. and to maintain her links with those churches in the West that had a part in her growth.

Ministers of the F.C.C.I. – at present the Rev. Prakash Kumar and the Rev. David John – adhere to the Westminster Confession of Faith, with two minor modifications. These concern the relationship between the church and the civil magistrate, modifications that relate to India's Constitution as a secular, democratic republic. There is no Hindi translation of the Confession. Elders therefore take vows to adhere to the Shorter Catechism. The version inherited from Seoni was more Urdu than Hindi, but David John has helped prepare a more thoroughly Hindi edition, which is used in Sunday Schools also. Premnagar has two elders, the elderly C. H. Gladwin, and a younger man, C. B. Kujur. Panna Lall and Samuel Masih are elders in Chhapara, the former at present acting as assessor elder for Lakhnadon. At the time of writing, the four congregations together have about one hundred members – Lakhnadon seventeen, Chhapara thirty-five, Premnagar thirty-five, and Vijainagar twelve.

"A good stewardship man" had been David John's reputation in the Church of North India. He sets a fine example by his own life-style and encourages others too to give beyond the tithe. The Foreign Missions' Board currently provides 66% of the church workers' salaries. It also paid in recent years for the land bought at Vijainagar and for part of the building costs. One third was borne locally. The same holds for the new church in Chhapara – the congregation is responsible for one third of expenses. Since the older centres are rural and the newer ones urban, there is potential for good interchange and mutual support between Lakhnadon, Chhapara, Premnagar and Vijainagar – potential yet to be realised.

The F.C.C.I., like its mother church in Scotland, follows the regulative principle in worship – that only what has an express warrant in Scripture may be introduced into public worship. When in 70 A.D. the Temple in Jerusalem was destroyed, as Jesus had foretold, its way of worship, with animal sacrifices and musical instruments, was superseded. Not until we come to the book of Revelation at the end of the New Testament do we read of trumpets and harps again. Prone as we are now to take pride in our own inventions, we find it good to use our voices only in singing praise at public worship.

The Psalms, superb as songs of worship, were imprisoned for too long in the Urdu language before coming into Hindi. Throughout North India in the nineteenth century and into the twentieth, Urdu was the language of the church's liturgy, probably because its concepts are nearer those of the Judeo-Christian traditions than are Hindi's. But Hindi is now the language of the people. Men of the Seoni church transliterated the Urdu Psalter into Roman script and then into the Deva-Nagari, which is that used for Hindi. A Lewis lady, Miss Mary Macaulay, visiting Lakhnadon in 1961, subsidised the cost of supplying this latest edition in the Free Church area. It could be read by anyone literate in Hindi, but the meaning was not clear. Although there is considerable overlap between the two languages as now spoken in North India, the vocabulary used was too heavily Urdu. All metres and tunes were from the West. The Geelong congregation of the Presbyterian Church of Eastern Australia financed further progress.

Ian McKenzie began collecting Hindi translations of Psalm portions, set to Indian tunes. Fifteen of these were introduced, to the delight of some but the disapproval of others more loyal to Seoni traditions. Donald MacDonald and David John worked hard to produce more. In 1987 a new Hindi Psalter appeared with one hundred and thirty portions representing eighty-five Psalms. Some of them retain Western rhythm and tune (now firmly adopted by Indian Christians), while some are more Eastern. Mrs Taramoni Lall, wife of evangelist Mr Panna Lall and nursing sister in charge of Chhapara Christian Health Centre, has composed songs on health topics, set to simple tunes. They are easily learnt and remembered by even illiterate villagers. She smiled when I suggested that the wonderful truths of God's Word – say Psalm 117 – might be communicated in this way. The new Hindi Psalter is a vast improvement on the old one. But it still lacks a uniformly authentic Indian flavour, which Mrs Lall's songs have. Many Indian people are deep thinkers who, listening to simple lyrics telling the basics of the Christian faith, dismiss it all as too simplistic. We need the wide sweep of the Psalms to teach of God's greatness, his holiness and his loving concern for his whole creation. A clearer vision to communicate the knowledge of God in Christ to ordinary people of Hindu

गीत ३६

[भजन संहिता ३७:१-९] सी. एम.

१ कुकर्मियों के कारण से तू मन में कुछ न कुढ़,
   कुटिलता करने वालों से तू मन में डाह न कर ।

२ वे घास की नाईं जल्दी से काट डाले जाएंगे,
   और हरी घास ही के समान काट डाले जाएंगे ।

३ यहोवा पर भरोसा रख और सदा भला कर,
   देश में निवास कर अपना मन लगा सच्चाई पर ।

४ तब तू प्रभु यहोवा में, आनन्दित रहेगा,
   वह तेरे मनोरथों को पूरा कर देवेगा ।

५ तू अपने मार्ग की चिंता यहोवा को सौंप दे,
   उसी पर तू भरोसा रख वह करेगा पूरे ।

६ तेरे धर्म को वह ज्योति सा प्रगट कर देवेगा,
   तेरा न्याय दोपहर समान प्रगट कर देवेगा ।

७ यहोवा के सम्मुख चुप रह आस्रा रख धीरज से,
   जब दुष्ट कामों में सफल हैं मत कुढ़ इस कारण से ।

८ क्रोध करने से तू अलग रह जलजलाहट छोड़ दे,
   मत कुढ़ क्योंकि बुराई ही निकलेगी उसी से ।

९ क्योंकि सब ही कुकर्मी लोग काट डाले जाएंगे,
   पर जो प्रभु की बाट जोहते जग पर राज्य करेंगे ।

गीत ४०

[भजन संहिता ४०:१-५]

कोरस-मैंने धीरज से यहोवा की प्रतीक्षा की,
   उसने मेरी ओर झुककर मेरी दोहाई सुनी ।

१ उसने मुझे दलदल में से उबारा, सत्यानाश के गड़हे में से
   उसने मुझे चट्टान पर खड़ा करके मेरे कदमों को दृढ़ किया है ।

२ उसने मुझे एक नया गीत सिखाया जो परमेश्वर की स्तुति का है
   बहुत लोग यह देखकर डरेंगे और प्रभु पर भरोसा रखेंगे ।

Parts of Psalms 37 and 40 in the Hindi Psalter.

and Muslim background might motivate makers of good music.

The Free Church of Central India, a tiny part of India's Christian community, considers the theological stance of the Church of North India too liberal. Yet she does not want to be isolationist. The Rev. David John serves on the Board of Management of the Theological Seminary of the Reformed Presbyterian Church in U.P. Emmanuel Peter of Chhapara, at present the F.C.C.I.'s one candidate for the ministry, is studying there. The F.C.C.I. is a member of the Hindi section of the Evangelical Fellowship of India, which links evangelicals in fellowship and witness. The church has also joined the Association for Theological Education by Extension (TAFTEE). Some of TAFTEE's excellent study material used by F.C.C.I. groups was produced by Robin Thomson, son of the Free Church missionary Anna Thomson, née Stewart, and her husband Cyril.

The F.C.C.I. has not yet joined the Federation of Evangelical Churches of India, a widely-based group of fifteen small bodies. Perhaps membership would carry no immediate benefits. But her two ordained ministers in particular, with their warm love to Christ and their understanding of Reformed truth, could contribute much to other churches.

Ever since Christian missionaries first came to India, and particularly in the state of Orissa in recent decades, **groups** of low-caste and tribal people have professed conversion to Christ. In some cases this seems to have been a movement for mainly social and/or economic reasons. Where animistic tribal people are not influenced by Hinduism they tend to be more genuinely responsive to the Gospel. In Seoni District Hindu influence is very strong. The Hindu majority dislikes any increase in the Christian minority community. The State Parliaments of both Madhya Pradesh and of Orissa have passed legislation to regulate profession of conversion. If a person decides to change his (or her) religion, he has to sign an Affidavit before a Magistrate declaring that he is doing so of his own free will, without pressure or bribery. The Christian pastor who administers baptism to such a person has to report details of it to the police within seven days. Usually there are no repercussions from government authorities.

However, repercussions are common in a convert's social life. Hindus may not object to a person's belief in Jesus Christ as long as he does not repudiate his caste. Born into a particular caste, in that caste he should remain all his life, they say. But baptism indicates a decisive step out of that system. Family and community may treat him as if he had died, to the extent of performing funeral rites for him. Only a member of such a community can know what this feels like. Land and inheritance are likely to be forfeited. He may have no means of livelihood left. If employment or other material help is then offered by Christians, suspicion of ulterior motives is strengthened.

Muslims are usually even fiercer in their opposition to one of their community who becomes a Christian. Early death may be considered his due, and arrangements made for it. In former times admission to the Muslim fold was often forcible. Now groups of people, as well as individuals, eager to escape from low-caste or tribal status, become Muslims or Buddhists voluntarily, just as some, mentioned above, may profess conversion to Christ from the same motive.

Of India's population of about eight hundred million 3% are classed as Christians. The majority of these live in the south and extreme north-east of the country. In Madhya Pradesh less than 1% are known as Christians, and most of these are Roman Catholics. As a result of God's grace seen in the quiet work by Free Kirkers in part of that state – work through service to people in need and through the preaching of the Word – a church exists. Our brothers and sisters in the Reformed faith, aware of their minority status, are tempted to withdraw from witnessing as individuals and as a body. But the Lord vindicates those who do not give way to fear or indifference. Let us remember them in prayer, as they remember us.

Emmanuel Peter.

During a visit in July and August 1988 to places where I had previously worked in India, Christian fellowship was enriching. Physically, many changes were obvious. Although the main roads of Madhya Pradesh are still as bumpy as ever – and no wonder, considering their constant pounding by massive trucks – side roads have improved greatly. Many villages as far as twenty miles from National Highway Seven are accessible almost all the year round. People who used to walk long distances to Chhapara or Lakhnadon have a bus service once or twice a day.

Safe drinking water is now available in a good number of villages. Bore wells about two hundred feet deep, a few inches wide and fitted with hand-pumps have been installed by the Government or by Christian charitable organisations. (Many disappointingly dry bores were also made.) Some people have yet to be convinced that this water is better than that from an open well, which is usually contaminated. The taste is different!

Preventive medicine is now more readily accepted, but is not available everywhere. Parents request immunisation for their children instead of refusing it. Even grandparents can be enthusiastic! Unfortunately, supplies of vaccine are not always reliable. Even when available, polio drops are useless unless kept on ice. A break in the "cold chain" from manufacturers to suppliers to distributors to users is all too common. Measles immunisation is still not widely available.

Television is watched by millions – another contrast to a few years ago. Sets are fitted above railway platforms as well as in shops and homes. The general tone of programmes seems higher than in Britain. Most is for entertainment. Some good programmes are educational. Popular Hinduism is often featured. The lure of entertainment from 5 p.m. on the Lord's Day may contribute to lower attendances at evening services. Materialism is no less a snare than in Free Church circles in Scotland. Many Christian families are now comfortably middle-class by local standards, taking television for granted.

India today is not a poor country. Her wealth, however, is unequally distributed. In spite of family planning, her population continues to rise. While a high standard of living (high by any standard) is enjoyed by the rich, millions in villages and urban slums live far below the poverty line. The middle classes, which scarcely existed in ancient times, are growing steadily in numbers and in influence.

Changes were obvious not only in the environment but in personnel also. The missionaries of today are nationals. Mr Arun K. Patras, Administrator at Lakhnadon Christian Hospital since 1979, was appointed Senior Administrative Officer by E.H.A. in place of Dr Donald MacDonald who left in 1988. He therefore has overall responsibility for the medical work and is Chairman of the Hospital Management Committee. Mr and Mrs Patras are Methodists. Since their three children stay with grandparents in Jabalpur in order that they may attend school there, the parents often spend time at weekends with them in the city. In the rural setting of E.H.A. hospitals, English-medium schools are scarce, a fact that can discourage senior staff from serving there long-term.

At Chhapara, Christian families have grown, the little ones of twenty-five years ago now being parents themselves. Mrs Taramoni Lall is as enthusiastic as ever in her large Sunday School. She teaches children and adults, some still illiterate, to pass on to others what they themselves learn. The school teachers invited me to join in their Bible study, led by the Rev. Prakash Kumar. And I saw a start made on houses for two young men who were orphans. Visiting Jabalpur, I was on ground less familiar to me, particularly in Vijainagar. But because of our oneness in Christ, there was no sense of strangeness.

Towards the end of my revisit to India in August 1988 I left Lakhnadon early one morning. The bus from Seoni to Jabalpur was late. Another lady waiting for it began to talk. A vegetable-seller, she was going to the city to buy a dozen sacks of potatoes. She would have them loaded on to a truck whose driver she knew and would then catch an evening bus back to Lakhnadon. Would I want potatoes in tomorrow's bazaar?

When she knew I had been visiting the Christian Hospital, I heard enthusiastic details of her experience of it – the terrible pain in her stomach, the good doctor's treatment and her gratitude for a full recovery. Eventually the bus came. As I travelled away from the centre of India towards Scotland I too was grateful, because village folk there are still being helped in Jesus' name.

And yet how few, how very few show evidence of a saving faith in him!

Satsang – an open discussion of religious topics, giving opportunity to speak of Christ.

what a Saviour!

At the time of writing in 1989, there are no missionaries from the Free Church of Scotland in India. Even so, service in the name of Christ continues. The latest successor to Dr Annie Mackay at Lakhnadon, an Indian doctor, might spend a typical week like this:

Sunday: *The doctor is called to the wards at 6 a.m. to see an asthmatic man admitted late last night. A slow intravenous injection gives great relief. The doctor with his wife and little girl are glad of a lift with others in the hospital jeep to the 8.30 a.m. church service. Today the preacher is Mr Panna Lall, who has come by bus from Chhapara. There are twenty at the service, the majority being hospital staff.*

Since all is in order when he does the ward-round before lunch, the doctor, who has no medical colleague to stand in for him, risks going to Chhapara where he has been asked to preach at the 4.30 p.m. service. It is good to share in the fellowship there, not least with the Rev. Prakash Kumar. Before the doctor returns to Lakhnadon, they exchange news and pray together. The weekly Bible study held at the Mission School is encouraging, as are visits to (nominally) Christian families of government employees at Chhapara. About twenty people, mostly young folk, came to the Saturday fellowship meeting, held last night in the minister's home. It was a friendly gathering. Some videos now available in Seoni show very low moral standards. Should Christians watch videos? There was useful discussion about Christian principles and conduct, with emphasis on the fact that Christ is not only Saviour but also Lord.

Back at Lakhnadon, the nurses have coped well with an unbooked maternity case. There were ten people at the evening service.

Monday: *After prayers in the wards and with staff, the doctor does two operations, one for hernia, one for hydrocele. With no senior nurse now on the staff, it is a heavy responsibility to ensure that all is safe for surgery.*

Bazaar day brings forty out-patients, with a variety of complaints – scabies, tuberculosis, bronchitis, anaemia, dysentery. A young woman, paralysed from the waist down for the last three months, is brought from a distant village. She has advanced Hodgkin's disease and has been treated already by many other practitioners. The doctor discusses the case with the family. They agree to go to Jabalpur Medical College Hospital for chemotherapy, and possibly radiotherapy also. But, with corruption all too common and money already wasted on other treatment, one cannot be confident that she will be greatly benefited now. She is admitted at Lakhnadon overnight while her relatives make arrangements for her to go to Jabalpur.

Tuesday being his day for Chhapara – a tradition from Dr Annie Mackay's era – the doctor spends extra time and care on the evening round.

Tuesday: *The driver is ready at 7 a.m. in the hospital car. They stop three miles north of Chhapara to pick up two patients. Three smiling women, village health workers, climb in too. Today the village health workers – commonly known as V.H.W.s – give their reports to Mrs Lall and stock up with basic remedies.*

It's a pleasure to come to the Chhapara Christian Health Centre. However much a doctor is respected, the **nurses** *are the really important people (next to the patients, of course) where health matters are concerned! Mrs Taramoni Lall sets a high standard herself and encourages others to do the same.*

The number and variety of out-patients are much as in Lakhnadon yesterday. Over lunch, the Lalls tell the doctor how the man admitted from a distant village for tuberculosis treatment is quick to learn health matters. He is giving good help in teaching others how to prevent disease, and goes out with the Community Health team.

From Chhapara the doctor goes on to Seoni. At the Government Hospital there, ample supplies of tetanus toxoid, Triple Antigen and polio drops are promised – all to be collected at Chhapara Primary Health Centre tomorrow. In spite of the official letter handed to him, the doctor has doubts. Will the vaccines materialise?

At Lakhnadon, patients have waited for him since morning and there are problems in the wards. It is 9 p.m. before the doctor can relax at home. Once again he has missed the mid-week prayer-meeting, held this evening in the home of one of the hospital drivers.

A snake-bite victim, admitted at midnight, has no symptoms or signs of poisoning – a great relief to all.

Wednesday: *Listening to the young man leading morning worship in the wards, the doctor wonders how better use might be made of this opportunity for witness. As usual, between the singing of a gospel lyric and the offering of prayer, a Bible passage telling of one of Jesus' miracles is read, with the brief comment that if we believe, all will be well. How to communicate clearly the good news of God's plan of salvation to those who are not aware of a* **holy** *God, nor of his love to sinners? How many understand what sin is? Are we Christians living in such a way that others will want to* **see Jesus** *too? Today the Administrator leads staff prayers. It is good to take this time to pray together. What a privilege it is for Christians to serve as a team in Jesus' name!*

Even so, difficulties there are in plenty. The lack of a senior nursing sister means lack of supervision for junior nurses. This can be hazardous. And cleaning *staff are slack in their work. Some relatives, who are men of influence in the area, have dropped dark hints to the nurses of what could happen if **their** patient is not given preferential treatment. The hospital generator, working long hours because of frequent electricity cuts, is showing signs of trouble. Repair will be costly. Hospital income is not keeping pace with expenditure at present.*

The Administrator has many concerns and the doctor shares them. But they can afford only a few minutes for discussion now. Ward round and out-patients are demanding attention.

At 1 p.m., just when staff are going for lunch, an old lady arrives. (Well, she must be over fifty!) She fell and broke her wrist last night. Her son asks anxiously about an X-ray. Yes, the machine is working, but no film is available. Yes, the fracture can be set later today. No, she won't be allowed home tonight, but tomorrow. As so often happens, these people of humbler means are cooperative. They give half the money asked for and will try to have the rest tomorrow. Although the doctor is delayed, he feels refreshed when he goes for lunch. He had taken advantage of the comparative quiet to share something of his hope in the living Saviour with a group of relatives.

During the afternoon, two visitors call at the Administrative Office. They are members of Lakhnadon Lions' Club. Over glasses of hot, sweet tea, brought from the food-stall just outside the hospital gate, they talk. Last year the Christian Hospital helped to staff a Diagnostic Camp in a village where Roman Catholics from South India work, about sixteen miles east of Lakhnadon. The doctor examined two hundred and fifty patients in one day. Simple remedies were prescribed for many and advice on further treatment given to those more seriously ill. Could the same be done again this year? The Administrator thinks so and promises to talk it over with the doctor.

When routine and emergency clinical work is finished at 7 p.m., the morning discussion is continued. If government supplies of vaccine do not materialise soon, it will be necessary to send someone to Nagpur to try and buy some there. That might take a few days if the suppliers have to wait for the next consignment coming by air from Madras. They decide which driver can be spared. Considering the Diagnostic Camp, they think it wise to cooperate again. And so the discussion goes on. It is good that their wives are patient ladies and that food has not spoiled by the time they eventually have their evening meal!

Thursday: *At 2 a.m. the doctor is called to see a maternity case just admitted. The patient needs immediate Caesarean section. Knowing his limitations, the doctor suggests transfer to Jabalpur after emergency treatment. But this family of Gondhs is adamant. They have always come here when anyone is ill. Why should they go elsewhere now? The risks are explained – limited theatre facilities, lack of blood transfusion. But they insist they want to stay. Encouraged by their confidence, the doctor agrees. The patient, accustomed to hard work in the fields, comes through the operation bravely. Their first son is born, alive and* *well. Rejoicing all round!*

Out-patients are fewer today, but one person is troublesome. He and his wife are government employees, one in an office, one a teacher. They have three children. If they have more, they will be penalised regarding privileges and promotion. Will the doctor oblige by terminating her fourth pregnancy? It takes a long time to convince the gentleman that in this Christian hospital such abortions have never been done, nor is there any intention of doing one now. They do not appreciate the reasons given. If the doctor's little girl were a few years older and a pupil in Lakhnadon, her schooling might well suffer from her father's refusal to oblige. As it is, threats of violence to him, hints of a gift if he agrees, all the arts of persuasion leave him with a sad heart but a clear conscience. Unfortunately, the termination will probably be done elsewhere.

The evening ward round is more relaxed than usual. Everyone knows about last night's hard work and success. Since walls have ears, people are aware too of the doctor's principled stand against abortion, and most admire him for it. Of the twenty-eight patients admitted at present, five are ready for discharge tomorrow. One man in a private room is most reluctant to go. His brother-in-law is involved in a court case just across the road next Monday. It is so convenient to be here!

Ramabai, a year-old girl weighing ten pounds, is recovering from acute gastroenteritis plus malnutrition. She should stay, but her parents must return to work in their fields and insist on going home tomorrow. Fortunately their village is one that has recently welcomed the Community Health team. The health worker being trained there will keep an eye on Ramabai and encourage the mother to **feed** the child. As the doctor leaves the ward, one of the helpers is called in. With a set of flip-charts, she gives a brief lecture in the local dialect about local weaning foods. No matter that she is illiterate. The message is clear to all who will listen.

Friday: The Community Health team of three, leaving early as usual, give a lift in the jeep to tiny Ramabai and her parents, since their village is on today's schedule.

Health education and immunisations are unspectacular work, involving much hard slog and little thanks. If the team were asked what they do, one might say, "Give injections"; another, "Train local women to encourage healthy habits"; and a third, "Share the love of God by showing that we care, especially for the poor". (Dr Raj Arole, Community Development pioneer in Maharashtra, says that, ten years after he and his wife began work in that drought-stricken area, people began asking for Bibles.) The team, hot and weary, return by lunch-time. In the afternoon, one attends to statistics, while others check up on supplies. The stock of vaccines is very low.

At the hospital, bazaar day has again brought dozens of patients. The registration clerk and the cashier, the lab. technician and the dispenser, the nurse *and the doctor – all are busy from morning to night. Some are late off duty. Then, if they did not manage down to the bazaar at lunch time, they have a quick trip on foot or cycle before dark to buy grain, vegetables and fruit.*

At 11 p.m. a man is brought in from a road traffic accident two miles away. His bullock cart, travelling without a light, was hit by a jeep. If the jeep had been travelling at speed, damage would have been far worse. After emergency treatment for a compound fracture of his right arm, he is referred to Jabalpur. The doctor sanctions the use of the hospital ambulance; the trip is paid for – after the patient's brother has visited a money-lending merchant in Lakhnadon bazaar – and away they go. The relatives of another patient have agreed to be responsible for the bullocks meantime and to salvage what is left of the cart, once the police give permission.

Saturday: *Today's theatre list is short – one tubectomy for a mother-of-five; one haemorroidectomy; incision and drainage of an enormous abscess, the result of an injection given elsewhere; and a new plaster for a lad with a month-old fracture of his left lower leg. The lady who had a Caesarean section on Thursday meets the doctor at the ward door when he goes for the round. She is tough!*

Clinic work is over by 1 p.m., and it looks like being a quiet afternoon. The Administrator and his wife are going to Jabalpur. There is hospital shopping to be done. Two off-duty nurses are going for the outing. The doctor is tempted to go too, with his wife and daughter. After finding out how last night's patient is in the orthopaedic ward of the Medical College Hospital, he could look up some of the medical students there. He used to have a Bible study with them every month or so when he was not the only doctor at the hospital. With his family, he could stay in the Premnagar manse guest-room and appreciate David John's ministry tomorrow. However, he decides against leaving the nurses without medical cover.

It is good to have time for some study. Consulting text-books about a puzzling case admitted this morning, he wonders how the hospital laboratory's inadequate facilities might be improved. After reading a medical journal, he writes to two friends. As medical students together, the three of them used to meet for prayer. One, who stayed on at their teaching hospital, is well on his way to gaining his post-graduate degree in General Surgery. The other joined an Indian missionary association. He and his wife, also a doctor, are pioneering gospel work in a very remote village of Madhya Pradesh. Thinking of his friends, the doctor is challenged afresh. Standards of clinical work, while appropriate to this forty-bed rural hospital, must not be allowed to slide. And he must resist the erosion of spiritual realities.

At family worship this Saturday evening, the doctor and his family wait on the Lord, who renews their strength and vision.

V AT HOME

'Understand what the Lord's will is.' [Eph. 5.17]

Room Eight.

The most obvious support to the work in India was given by the Church through the Foreign Missions' Committee/Board, which meets regularly in Room Eight of the Free Church of Scotland Offices on the Mound in Edinburgh. Less formal, but no less precious, was that given by women's groups, youth groups and individuals in congregations throughout Scotland and Northern Ireland, in Australia and North America.

14
Room Eight –
policy, finance and property

Aware that her reputation as a church was at stake, the Free Church of Scotland in 1900 appointed a Foreign Missions' Committee, since any church worthy of the name must engage in witness overseas. By 1924 she was responsible for fields in India, South Africa and Peru, as well as continental, colonial and Jewish work. Quite a spread for a small church, especially in the face of the economic depression of the 1920s and 1930s!

From 1900 until 1953 the Foreign Missions' Committee was like every other Standing Committee appointed by the General Assembly. Members served on the Committee for three years. There were only three 3-hour meetings each year. From 1953 it was allowed to meet six times per annum. Even so, an increasing volume and complexity of work demanded further change. In 1961 it was replaced by the Foreign Missions' Board.

Each year Presbyteries nominate persons to fill vacancies occurring on the Board (as they do also for the other Committees appointed by the General Assembly). The Nominations Committee puts forward the names of eight ministers and four elders. Final choice lies with the Assembly. At any one time each of the three Synods is represented by at least three members on the Board. Chairman and Vice-Chairman are appointed by the Assembly. Membership is for four years, but can be extended for a further four years. After that, a gap of at least a year must pass before re-appointment can take place. These new structures for the Board eased considerably the problems created by lack of continuity under the old Committee regulations.

In 1981 the Evangelical Presbyterian Church of Ireland was invited to appoint one representative to sit on the Board with the right to take part in all discussions but without a vote. The latter point is no great disadvantage since votes are rarely taken at Board meetings. Since 1988 the Editor of "From the Frontiers" has been an *ex officio* member.

The Board appoints its own Executive which meets as often as necessary to mature matters for decision and to deal with emergencies. Subcommittees give more detailed consideration to areas of special interest. A sub-committee's remit may be very limited and its work completed in a short time. Others continue in existence for several years. Some are a permanent feature of the Board's structure. The Board appointed an Indian Church Development Committee whose remit ran for several years until the Free Church of Central India was set up in 1986. The Recruitment and Personnel Committee, first set up in 1977, has an ongoing remit. A unique feature here is that now, with permission from the 1985 General Assembly, the Board co-opts to this sub-committee two **ladies** nominated by the W.F.M.A. Their status is advisory.

As the official link of the home church with the missionaries, the national churches and local institutions in the various countries, the Board has a wide area of responsibility.

In the days of the Foreign Missions' Committee, the frequent changes of personnel with the resulting lack of continuity led to consideration of the question of employing a permanent clerk. An increasing volume of secretarial work lent weight to this suggestion, but nothing resulted. In 1944 the conclusion of the Foreign Missions' Committee was, "The time is not ripe". In 1948 the General Assembly resolved to consider the appointment of a full-time secretary "at some future date". When the case was argued again in 1957 with strong pleas for better organisation and continuity, the Assembly deferred granting the request because "the cost would be prohibitive".

When the Board was set up in 1961 the post of Secretary was created. Not a member of the Board (and so without a vote), the Secretary serves long-term and therefore provides continuity. This was a significant step forward. Professor C. Graham (from 1961-79) and Professor A. C. Boyd (from 1979 to the present time) have both- "served the servants" with warm-hearted efficiency. However, any part-time secretary who has other heavy commitments in the Church would need to be superhuman to meet even the immediate demands of the Foreign Missions work.

The appointment of a full-time secretary was again debated at length in the Board meeting of December 1978. The consensus of opinion then was that the Church was "unprepared for such a new development". The 1979 General Assembly agreed with the Board to review the matter within five years. In 1979 the only change in organisation was the appointment of a secretary's assistant who would give priority to Foreign Missions business. Miss Christina MacIver is an excellent assistant, dealing with a large volume of clerical work, travel and deputation arrangements. But other responsibilities prevent her also from giving full attention to Foreign Missions business. The review in 1984 resulted in no change. One wonders for how long the overload will be ignored.

As far as I am aware, the Free Church has not spelled out its remit to the Foreign Missions' Committee/Board this century. In theory, the Board advises the General Assembly, which then forms policy. The Board's function is to carry out that policy. But in practice, the Board itself agonises over policy.

The objective of establishing an indigenous church has never been disputed as policy. Implicit in every report from missionaries and in every Foreign Missions Report to the General Assembly is a longing for God-glorifying fruit. Reading about the sixteen years of Murray Macleod's service (1933-49), one gets the impression of a promising response to a culturally-adapted presentation of the gospel, when precious truths were being made plain to Christian and non-Christian. Duncan Leitch's report (1955) breathes the same sense of urgency, to work and pray so that groups of believers would be established – groups where worship of the risen Lord, Bible teaching, fellowship and witness would be the norm. So, in the middle of this century, there was clearly a policy of church-planting, and the situation cried out for detailed strategy. But policy can be put into effect only if there are sufficient people to do the job. Unfortunately enough men with suitable gifts were not sent to India; nor did local leaders emerge in strength.

During the first half of the twentieth century, the situation was a totally **mission** one, without formal church organisation. The Foreign Missions' Committee operated in India through the Field Council. Although there was provision for national members, it was usually composed of expatriate missionaries only, colleagues from Seoni being coopted as necessary.

Soon after Independence in 1947, it became a legal requirement that all property-holding organisations should register with the government. In 1953 the Free Church of Scotland Mission Council, its membership identical with that of the Field Council, was registered with the Registrar of Firms and Societies at Nagpur, the capital city of Central Provinces. After a few years, state boundaries were altered. Seoni replaced Chhindwara as district headquarters. Seoni District is now part of Madhya Pradesh whose state capital is Bhopal. Immediately after the Annual General Meeting each year the Field Council Secretary must submit to the Registrar details of all office-bearers. With the arrival of five new missionaries between 1960 and 1965, seven of the eight names then on the list were of foreigners.

By 1970 few new missionaries were being allowed into India, and by 1984 virtually none. This helped hasten the process of transfer to Indian leadership. In 1986 the constitution of the Mission Council was altered, so that without expatriates it continues to function as an interim organisation. It is being replaced by three bodies – the Lakhnadon Christian Hospital Society, the Free Church Mission Education Society, and the Free Church of Central India. At the time of writing, in 1989, registration of the first and third of these has yet to be finalised.

Since 1976 there has been a strict curb on the entry into India of foreign money. The Foreign Contributions Regulation Act requires that details be given of source, amount, destination, user and use of cash from abroad. Prevention of misuse for purposes of subversion is the reason given. The amount of paperwork involved is enormous! One hopes that money now received from the West will help strengthen the church and para-church organisations, and will not merely cushion decline.

Closely connected with policy is this matter of finance. Until the Central Fund of the home church was set up in the 1970s the Foreign Missions' Board puzzled over both income and expenditure before submitting its budget each year. Under the more recently adopted procedures the Board (like any other Committee) is required to submit to the Finance, Law and Advisory (F.L.A.) Committee each October a budget for the following year. On the basis of these budgets, carefully scrutinised and often trimmed by the F.L.A. Committee, target figures are prepared for each congregation in the Church at home. The F.L.A. Committee is sympathetic, recognising the special difficulties faced by the Board in preparing its budget. Currency fluctuations; dramatic political and economic changes in countries of service; changing travel costs; and uncertainties about whether new recruits will be found and, if found, whether they will get visas – all these contribute to the difficulty of Board budgeting. Part of the Board's expenditure is met by the interest on investments made in the name of Foreign Missions.

Cooperating churches in Ireland, Australia and North America send money regularly to the Free Church Offices in Edinburgh for overseas mission work. Some have paid the salaries of missionaries recruited from their own membership.

Some interesting statistics of the percentage of her income that the Free Church spent on foreign missions during this century are given on page 168. The numbers of full-time missionaries employed are included too. India's share is noted separately; as is that of Asian Outreach.

Like other denominational missions, the Free Church has invested in property. In 1953 all property was registered under the Field Council. Because of political pressure within India, it was decided in 1973 to arrange that the Evangelical Trust Association of South India hold all properties for the church. Now this Trust holds land and buildings associated with the medical work on behalf of the Lakhnadon Christian Hospital Society. It holds those of the School in Chhapara for the Free Church Mission Education Society; and others for the Mission Council, an interim body (successor to the Field Council) due to be disbanded when the Free Church of Central India is registered, and when there is no further need of Orphanage funds.

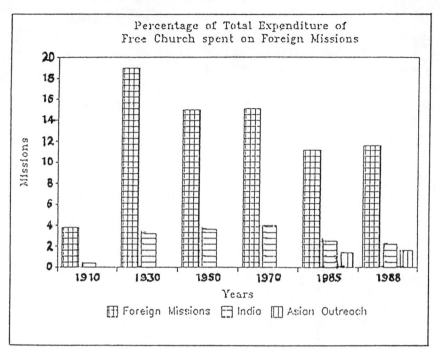

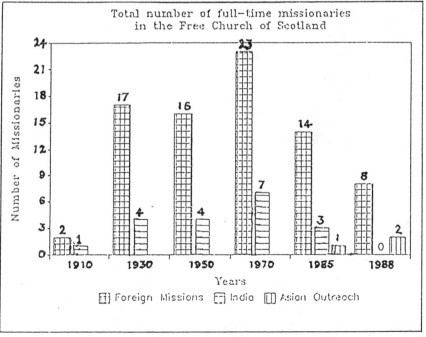

from a warm heart

Extract of a letter post-marked "Rogart, Sutherland" and dated 14th December 1966, from the Chairman of the Foreign Missions' Board to the Secretary of the Field Council at Lakhnadon:

..... *I submitted your correspondence and Field Council Minutes to a meeting of the Board held yesterday.*

The Board were glad to learn that the Lakhnadon buildings had been completed and opened, leaving a considerable balance in hand. They were gratified to know that you were able to meet part of the cost of furniture from monies received by way of gifts. What yet remains to be purchased may be paid for from the surplus funds in hand.

The Board's Executive was instructed to review the plans for the proposed Chhapara development. I would be glad to have all the relevant information that the Field Council can give.

The Board authorised that £100 be sent to India for the purchase of an autoclave .....

The Board endorsed the arrangements which had been made for your furlough. Please indicate if you wish the fare-money to be sent out. May God prosper you in everything and bring you safely to our shores.

You may have heard that our Irish friends have offered to provide the funds for a mobile dispensary for Chhapara. The Board have gratefully accepted their offer. The order is being placed with Mr Dewar, Stonehaven, who was so helpful with the Lakhnadon vehicle.

I trust you and your colleagues are well. It gives us great satisfaction to know that you are enjoying the facilities and comfort of the new buildings.

With warmest regards,

Yours very sincerely,

John R. Aitken
Chairman, Foreign Missions' Board

15
Room Eight –
in touch with people

Keeping in touch is also a Board responsibility. This is a two-way process. There is the duty not only to arrange for missionaries on leave to visit the home congregations, but also to keep in touch with the fields both by regular correspondence and by visiting them. On this last point the record as far as India is concerned was very poor.

During the first half of the twentieth century, no member of the Foreign Missions' Committee visited India. Were there really fewer problems in India than in South Africa or Peru? At the 1950 General Assembly, the Foreign Missions' Convener insisted that lack of policy demanded that two deputies visit India. This was rejected because it was said that the expense involved would discourage givings in Scotland. We may well ask to whose voice the Fathers and Brethren were listening!

Missionaries continued to plead for a visit and in 1954 the Rev. Duncan Leitch went to Lakhnadon, with good results. Even so, seventeen more years elapsed until, in 1971, the Board decided that all fields must be visited regularly, that is, at least once in five years.

The second deputation (of Chairman and Secretary) went to India in 1972 and made recommendations that have had far-reaching effects. From that time, all major decisions have been taken only after full consultation in India and in Scotland. The benefits of regular visitation are no longer questioned.

PERSONNEL

The 1908 General Assembly gave a remit to the Foreign Missions' Committee concerning "the recruitment and training of candidates, both male and female, to be its agents abroad". The Committee reported back in 1909 that no arrangement had been made. Their statement has a curious ring: "When, through perfecting of organisation, the special requirements of foreign missions would be more apparent, agents would then be found". If they were trying to avoid facing up to the necessity for recruitment and training, then they succeeded to a large extent. Occasionally during the twentieth century, particular individuals were approached by a member of Committee with a request to consider the claims of India. The response was negative in almost every case. Missionaries on home-leave were more successful in finding new colleagues. By the time a Recruitment and Personnel Committee was set up in 1977, India was not in a position to benefit.

Of course, recruitment is not the responsibility of the Board alone. Attention should be given throughout the church to Biblical preaching and teaching that challenges, motivates and equips people to go with the gospel. How much does the church corporately plead with God to thrust out labourers into the harvest fields? And, when it comes to the crunch, how willing are congregations, Kirk Sessions and Presbyteries to "lose" their best men to the wider work of the church?

Throughout the century, most candidates have offered their services spontaneously. In the 1920s and 1930s some nurses and a teacher were rejected because money was scarce. Others – a poultry instructress, a pharmacist, an agriculturalist – were turned down because their secular skills were considered inappropriate at the time. Still others were accepted and sent out with surprising speed. Why do we say surprising? In any enterprise, it is usual to train a worker!

The idea of training missionaries has been raised time and again. The editor of "The Monthly Record" in April 1933 advised that "wise mission boards will ensure that their candidates are given the best all-round training". There was some training – in relation to professional skills. One nurse, for example, might be required to take midwifery training before leaving for India; another, training in tropical medicine or administration while on home-leave.

The 1955 General Assembly directed the Foreign Missions' Committee to make provision for a course of training for unordained missionaries. This was passed on to the Executive Committee. Act VIII of the 1962 General Assembly states that the Free Church of Scotland **"selects, appoints and sends forth"** certain categories of missionary. There is no mention of training.

In August 1964 the Board noted that some of its members recommended training for unordained candidates. When the matter was brought up in the next General Assembly, the Chairman gave the assurance that the Board was "not unaware of the matter". It was "kept in mind"; but all their "missionaries were from good homes". Apparently he meant that they did not require training since their upbringing was largely sufficient. The request for training was repeated two years later in the Assembly. Missionaries on home-leave expressed a sense of need. Although in 1977 it was decided "to arrange basic theological education for those whose preparation had not included it", nurses returning from India in 1978 and 1984 were not encouraged to study within the Free Church. Both went to the Bible Training Institute in Glasgow.

However, the need was for more than teaching in Reformed theology. Even ordained men need training to live and work effectively in a different climate and culture. To benefit from Orientation Studies at Language School in India, it was necessary to struggle free from the mentality, "The way we're used to doing it must be best". Help in coping with a different culture and language can greatly ease the difficulties faced by a new missionary. Being aware of the adjustments and changes needed in a different cultural context will maximise a person's contribution. It **is** possible for cross-cultural communication to be learned the hard way, by trial and error. But lack of training and preparation is more likely to result in a ministry insensitive to the people contacted – a contact therefore greatly impaired in its usefulness. During the 1980s several Free Church missionary recruits have benefited from orientation courses of The Evangelical Alliance Relief agency.

Once in India, how did missionaries fare?

In December 1963 the Chairman and Secretary published a joint appeal in "The Monthly Record": "Provision for families' education, for medical aid in sickness, for pensions on retirement – these things are mooted, discussed and shelved for lack of funds. Must it always be so?" That appeal reveals the situation that had existed for so many years. While single persons in robust health used their surplus on good causes locally, families were often in financial straits. Allowances for health care; for holidays; for travel; for children's food, clothing and education were minimal, and were usually labelled *"ex gratia"*. Men of independent mind hesitated to ask for more. If a request was made, lack of funds in Scotland could provoke a defensive response: "Bide by the terms of your contract". But after the 1963 appeal, the records show considerable improvement in the financial lot of missionaries.

Fixing of salaries has not always been straight-forward. The yard-stick is the Equal Dividend, the stipend paid to ministers at home. This is usually paid to ordained missionaries, male doctors and male teachers. Lady missionaries were paid a percentage of this, doctors receiving a higher percentage than nurses, and they in turn more than Biblewomen. Some ladies negotiated a drop in salary, from a variety of motives. In the 1930s they were helping lessen the Foreign Missions' Committee's debt. They grudged paying heavy Indian income tax in the 1960s; and by the 1980s there was a concern to be more on a level with national colleagues. The Board reckons, with hind-sight, that this was a doubtful expedient. For one thing, it disguised the real cost of maintaining the Indian work.

As always, when payment is made in the home-country's currency, exchange rates alter the value of a salary. The pound reached its lowest ebb in the late 1970s, when it was worth only thirteen rupees, compared with twenty-four at other times. Even so, Free Church missionary families during the seventies and eighties fared well compared with those in the hungry forties. National Insurance contributions for missionaries have been paid by the home church since 1955.

The appointment of a Secretary to the Board, even although only part-time, has made it possible to give more attention to the differing circumstances of missionaries and their families. For example, in the area of home-leave, individuals differ in their preference regarding frequency of furlough. One appreciates brief leave more often, to see young nephews and nieces before they grow out of recognition, or to minimise disruption of work. Another prefers to stay long enough on the field to earn twelve months in Scotland, because this allows children a full session at school in the home country. Also, the unfolding of four seasons at home is in refreshing contrast to Central India's abrupt three. Since missionaries would now be seconded to work with Indian organisations, coordination with these bodies is necessary.

PUBLICITY

Publicity is important for the ongoing support of the work. Prayer, giving and the challenge to possible new recruits all benefit from a regular flow of information. The home churches are the Presbyterian Church of Eastern Australia, the Evangelical Presbyterian Church of Ireland, the Free Church of Scotland and its Synod in North America. The Foreign Missions' Board aims to keep these churches and other funding agencies well informed.

From 1949 to 1980, a major rôle in communication was played by the quarterly magazine "From the Frontiers". For fifteen years its editorship was delegated to ladies in the church. From 1964 until 1980 the Board's Secretary took on that responsibility. Throughout this century both "The Monthly Record" and "The Instructor" have carried news and articles on overseas work. The volume and frequency of these items depended on the enthusiasm of the editors and the readiness of various contributors. Since the suspension of the quarterly "From the Frontiers", "The Monthly Record" has included under the same title four pages specifically relating to overseas work. The editor of these four pages edits an annual missions magazine also with the same name.

Various other sporadic attempts have been made at publicity. In 1949 a 72-page booklet, "Missionary Endeavour", was published by the Foreign Missions' Committee. It told the story of work in three continents during the first half of the century. From 1926 to 1956, copies of the Foreign Missions' Report to the General Assembly were printed separately, and sold. This and, from 1942 to 1955, the production of a calendar which featured a person or scene from India, Africa or Peru, brought in much-needed cash. In the mid-sixties, the Board published a small booklet about each of its three fields. The Indian one contained Ram Das' story, related at the beginning of this book. The Board now promotes literature put out by the Emmanuel Hospital Association about medical work in India. A video about E.H.A. is also available.

The part-time secretaries and editors just do not have the time necessary to ensure the production of regular up-to-date publicity materials. The appointment of a full-time secretary could ensure both an improved flow of publicity materials and a better use of what is available.

In addition to the printed page, publicity is accomplished by people, in person. Prominent Free Churchmen represent us interdenominationally. Dr Alexander Stewart was a delegate to the 1910 World Missionary Conference in Edinburgh. Alexander Dewar, a Free Church missionary in South Africa, addressed the Scottish Churches' Missionary Campaign at Glasgow in 1922. The Free Church became a member of the Evangelical Missionary Alliance in 1962, and the Secretary to the Foreign Missions' Board of the Free Church attended the Reformed Ecumenical Synod Missionary Conference in 1968.

In 1985 the first full meeting of the International Conference of Reformed Churches (I.C.R.C.), at Edinburgh, appointed a Committee on Missions with a remit to investigate possibilities of cooperation in missionary work. The Secretary of the Free Church of Scotland Foreign Missions' Board was appointed Chairman of that committee. The report presented to the I.C.R.C. Conference in Vancouver in June 1989 identified current activities and future plans of member churches, and gave their views on possible cooperation. Its Missions' Committee's remit now reflects its concern for progress in missionary training by member churches and for publication of material on the methodology of mission.

The Emmanuel Hospital Association European Fellowship, which promotes E.H.A.'s interests in Western Europe, has a representative of the

Foreign Missions' Board on its main committee.

Some missionaries on home leave dread Thursday evening of Assembly week, when the Foreign Missions slot includes their addresses to the Fathers and Brethren. They have been known to adjust travel plans so as to avoid Edinburgh during the third week of May! Many visitors regard Thursday evening as the highlight of the week. Missionaries **do** appreciate the warmth of the welcome they are given. But it is difficult, in an atmosphere of uncritical review and within the limited time available, to have helpful discussion following the Chairman's Report. Christians from India would be the first to ask that the work there should not be treated like a sacred cow, revered too highly to be criticised. In the past, ignorance of conditions in faraway places may have made people hesitate to venture an opinion. Such ignorance is now without excuse.

Regular programmes of deputation are arranged for missionaries on home leave. Annual Youth Conferences and Spring (Study) Conferences give opportunity for less formal contacts. During the 1960s, Aberdeen hosted a Missionary Exhibition, and Free Church missionaries took part. Presbyteries of our church sometimes arrange a series of meetings or one central gathering, with a particular person on home leave as speaker. Since 1984 Missionary Conferences arranged at Presbytery level have been held in Dornoch, Dingwall, Inverness, Edinburgh and Glasgow. Lasting for two or three days, they provide a varied programme. The involvement in such meetings of Board members as well as missionaries opens up more possibilities of publicity. In this area also there is great potential for a full-time secretary, although the appointment of mission coordinators in several Presbyteries has greatly helped. Women may prefer to address a group of ladies only. Too often this is the only type of meeting arranged – surely an indication of scant interest among other members of that congregation.

From 1956 the Evangelical Union of South America held its annual conference in St Andrews jointly with the Free Church. At least one representative of the Free Church Foreign Missions' Committee attended, sometimes as speaker; and missionaries from all our fields were welcome. Only once, at Larbert in 1984, has a get-together been arranged specifically for all Free Church missionaries on home-leave, with wives and children, and Board members. It was voted a great success. The fewness of missionaries in Scotland at any one time makes it difficult to arrange such a get-together on a regular basis. Male missionaries attending the School of Theology, held each autumn since the 1950s, have had their fees paid by the Committee/Board. They benefit themselves, and contribute to the deliberations. Sometimes an ordained missionary on home leave preaches in a congregation that has no settled minister, as in 1947 when Murray Macleod and his family were in Scotland for two years because of illness.

He supplied the Inverness pulpit for many months, resulting in good fruit that lasts until today.

Two ordained men from the Free Church in India have visited Scotland. The Rev. Prakash Kumar came in 1974 and the Rev. David John in 1985. It was a pleasure for many to meet and to hear these men. There is a risk of keeping such visitors so busy with meetings that they have little opportunity of observing the regular working of a congregation. Such an opportunity might prove to be the kind of in-service training that would benefit all concerned. It has been suggested that more profit might result if visitors from our sister-churches abroad and missionaries on home-leave would stay for several weeks or months in one parish, rather than having a whirlwind tour of many. It is good to be flexible with arrangements, making allowances for differing gifts and needs. Recently a missionary who had returned after several years on the field spent six months as assistant in a home congregation before being settled in his own charge. The experience certainly helped the congregation to be even better informed about overseas work.

Benefits of holiday allowance – service with a smile to tired missionaries at a guest house in the hills.

snippets

November 1945: Glad when, through influences at home, school and church, am able to believe Isaiah 1:18, "Though your sins be as scarlet, they shall be as white as snow ..... "

March 1952: After secondary schooling, what? If Medicine (which seems the obvious thing), then might end up in India. Not sure that I want that!

February 1956: During fourth year of medical studies, am made willing for India. A sermon on Mark 8:34 makes plain the principle of following the Lord whatever the cost.

November 1961: Startled when my tentative enquiry about service in Lakhnadon is taken as final.

July 1966: Sad at something I've realised today. Many Indian people see sacrificial service in Orphanage, School or Hospital as the Christian's way of earning his own salvation.

May 1968: No escape from Thursday evening of Assembly week in Edinburgh! Still, the medical locums of recent months, useful in themselves, did let me off the hook of deputation work in Scotland.

June 1971: Realise now that I should have been more explicit in asking the Board for permission to go home before our mother died. Two months ago I heard that she was very weak. In a letter accompanying Field Council Minutes I hinted at the possibility of compassionate leave. The hint was not taken – my own fault. Now it's too late.

January 1973: Amazed at sense of security during motor-cycle accident. Timing of mail is good – Christmas card of a Highland glen and a postcard of snowdrops arrive right on time to cheer up a rather dreary hospital room in M.P. And could tapes of classical music ever be appreciated more?

September 1975: *Again amazed at God's over-ruling. When in Delhi en route to holiday in Kashmir, receive word of our father's serious illness. Am able to telephone home. (One and only call in more than twenty years!) "Come."*
But *my Foreigners' Registration is with the Superintendent of Police in Daltonganj, Bihar; and Income Tax documents are in M.P. One after another Government official in Delhi says "Impossible" to my request to leave the country without the correct papers. E.H.A.'s Secretary accompanies me on a determined and prayerful round of offices.*
Home within three days, a week before our father passes on.
Between arriving off the London-Edinburgh Shuttle flight and leaving Waverley by train for Inverness, I was relieved to be greeted sympathetically by the Board Secretary, without criticism for a hasty trip. The W.F.M.A. Secretary also came to see me at the station. On the train, I wished I had asked her to lend me a coat! Instead, to warm me up, I persuaded a sturdy little girl to sit on my lap.

January 1981: *Very puzzled. In 1976 my service in Kachhwa was supposed to be for several months. Now I feel I belong. In 1978, when visiting Lakhnadon, I packed household things in a trunk to bring to Kachhwa. But, on my way, was advised in Jabalpur (where a Board delegate was visiting) to send it back, which I did. Now my annual enquiry to Edinburgh, "How long may I stay in Kachhwa?" is again answered, "One more year". I often hear myself humming "This world is not my home" (in Hindi), and "Lord, THOU hast been our dwelling place" (in English).*

December 1982: *Angry, very angry, when yet another young bride, terribly burnt, is brought to us at Kachhwa on her way to Benares Hindu University Hospital. How long will this cruel dowry system persist? It's already outlawed by Parliament. But in practice it still endangers teenage wives if their in-laws are dissatisfied with what the girls' parents have paid. Oh, such horrendous suffering, caused so deliberately with paraffin and a match!*

June 1984: *Emergency trip from Kachhwa to Chhapara in the hottest of the hot weather. Comforting to be given kind hospitality by the Rev. Prakash Kumar and his family. Very good to feel one of them.*

December 1989: *Enormous relief to hand over the draft of this Indian story.*

16

In Homes, Church Halls and the Hebrew Classroom

Ministers of religion in Scotland are regarded as leaders in the church by virtue of their office. It is therefore encouraging when missionary interest is high among students in the Free Church College. Members of the Missionary Society there, meeting in the Hebrew classroom, produced a slim magazine, "The Macedonian Cry", in 1926. A second edition followed in 1929 and another in 1939. In 1932 their publication, "The Challenge of our Heritage", was of larger size and scope. Sale of these magazines boosted funds for foreign missions. They make interesting reading even today. All students are automatically members of the Missionary Society and the College has occasionally been a recruiting ground for India. But membership of a Missionary Society is not the same as serious consideration of any missionary challenge. Possibly concern for physical security is stronger than we think in this materialistic age.

Among women of the Scottish church, organised support of missions abroad began as early as 1821, with the formation of the Lanark Ladies' Auxiliary Society. The wife of John Wilson (a Scottish Missionary Society missionary, later of the Free Church of Scotland) and her two sisters pioneered education for girls in Bombay in the mid-nineteenth century. The Edinburgh Ladies' Association for the Advancement of Female Education in India was formed in 1837 in response to an appeal by a soldier, John Jameson. Returned from service in India, he gave a graphic account of the complete absence of schooling for poorer girls there and of the oppression of women in general. The Scottish Ladies' Association grew from the 1837 body and then gave way to the Women's Foreign Missionary Association. They recruited, sent out and supported their own lady missionaries, who worked in coordination with the Free Church Foreign Missions' Committee. Up to 1900 there had been 112 sent out. At the end of the nineteenth century, their recruits were receiving appropriate training at special courses held in the Edinburgh branch of the Young Women's Christian Association.

After 1900, women in the continuing Free Church organised work parties, sending to Seoni each year boxes packed with garments, blankets and toys. In January 1908 a sub-committee of the Foreign Missions' Committee reported that to revive the W.F.M.A. was inadvisable at that time "because of temporary exigencies". In March the matter was reviewed. As a result, Presbytery Clerks were advised to see that W.F.M.A. groups were formed again. On 21st May 1908 the ladies themselves got together and requested that they be allowed to form a Ladies' Missionary Association whose activities would include philanthropic work at home as well as abroad. The Foreign Missions' Committee pressed that it should be the Women's **Foreign** Missionary Association, and it was reconstituted as such in 1910. But the 1911 General Assembly decided to enlarge its scope. It then became the Foreign Missionary Association of the Free Church of Scotland. Its Convener and Vice-Convener were those of the Foreign Missions' Committee, while its executive committee was formed of ladies only.

Ladies collected money for foreign missions in their own congregations, handing the funds over to the Deacons' Courts. They continued to send mission boxes abroad. From 1911 until 1914 a lively little magazine, "The Foreign Missions Quarterly", was published. Edited by one of the honorary secretaries, Mrs Mackenzie of the Free North Manse, Inverness, it had a circulation of almost three thousand by the time it ceased publication soon after the outbreak of the First World War. At that time there were forty-seven branches of the Foreign Missionary Association, which means that about one third of the church's settled congregations had a branch. This is comparable to the strength of the W.F.M.A. today. In 1917 the Foreign Missions' Committee urged all Presbyteries to encourage the formation of an Association in every congregation. Even so, by 1926 the number had dropped to thirty-seven.

From 1926 until 1934 reports of activities at home related to foreign missions appear under a variety of names. We read of the annual general meeting of the Women's Missionary Association being held on 5th June 1926. "The Monthly Record" in 1927 and 1932 listed the names of those holding office in the Foreign Missionary Association. As in 1911, the Foreign Missions' Committee Convener and Vice-Convener held the same office in both bodies and the Foreign Missionary Association's executive committee had ladies only as its members. In 1928 the Glasgow Free Church Missionary Association advertised its meetings, inviting all who cared to join the young people on alternate Thursday evenings in Hope Street Church. A meeting of Inverness Ladies' Mission Association was held on 26th September 1933. But from 1934 onwards we read only of the Women's Foreign Missionary Association.

W.F.M.A. groups tend to have a core of ladies, not all middle-aged or older, who are genuinely concerned for the work of the Lord. Activities vary. Worship and prayer are important – prayer with the definite purpose of supporting national Christians and missionaries against evil forces. Small informal sales – of sewing, knitted goods, baking, pot-plants and so on – convert hours of their time and work into cash for mission. Some write letters to those prayed for – a real treat to get a letter you didn't expect, especially if it tells of ordinary interesting happenings at home and has notes of a meaty sermon! Visits by missionaries on home-leave and occasionally a visit by a W.F.M.A. member to the missionary abroad cement these valuable friendships.

Regular notes of items for prayer concerning all fields have been compiled by a W.F.M.A. member eight times a year since 1973. A word from the Foreign Missions Board Chairman in 1984 caused their heading to change from "W.F.M.A.'s" to "Free Church Missionary Prayer Notes". Over the years the number produced has grown from five hundred to nearly two thousand five hundred sets. From 1989 staff at the Offices in Edinburgh photocopy and send them out for use by individuals, families and congregations.

Representatives come from many parts of Scotland to the W.F.M.A.'s Annual General Meeting on the Thursday afternoon of Assembly week in May each year. Reports are given, business discussed and matters decided. Speakers bring greetings and news from overseas. Another meeting, on the Saturday afternoon of Assembly week, was discontinued in 1986. Since the 1920s, when Elizabeth Macleod and her colleagues needed a bullock cart (plus bullocks!) to take them out to distant villages, specific items or projects have been financed by the ladies of the church. In India we received food parcels and a regular supply of dried yeast from ladies in Vancouver, until Customs duty became excessive. Detroit gave money for a large tent in 1961, and Toronto for mattresses in the new Orphanage of 1969. An enormous amount of good has been done and is being done through the W.F.M.A. Long may it continue!

India has benefited from the interest of young people also. "The

Instructor" has encouraged them at various times to contribute for a hospital, its equipment, a wall and a well, among other items. Sponsored activities have raised money. Visits of nurses and medical students to Lakhnadon have been a good way of increasing awareness of opportunities abroad. At least one such visitor is now a missionary in Africa. The Edinburgh Missionary Youth Fellowship stimulated interest for about twenty years from the mid-1950s. The members sent out occasional prayer letters, and not a few became missionaries themselves.

A former missionary in Peru was responsible in 1945 for bringing out a pamphlet with the names of all Free Church missionaries, to encourage regular prayer. Some fifteen years later a small booklet, and in 1966 a larger edition, called "Labourers Together" was published by a group of young people in Glasgow. It gave a brief history of each field, with a map, names and pictures of national Christians as well as missionaries, and some details of the work. From the early years of the century, groups of Free Church people have met on Saturday evenings to pray for gospel witness abroad as well as at home. Dr John Cairns Christie, who died in 1973 at the age of 93 years, vigorously encouraged this practice. But congregations that travail regularly in prayer for mission work abroad are in a minority. One contrast I have noticed on returning home each time from India is the apparent neglect in the home church of the Bible's promises about the fervent believing prayer of righteous people. Difficult situations cropped up constantly in India. We were driven to God in urgent prayer. He proved faithful time after time. It is good at the time of writing to be aware of a burden among young people in Edinburgh to seek the Lord in prayer.

Yet on the whole, young people are amazingly ignorant of what is going on in Peru, Southern Africa and India. And older folk are not much better. Admittedly publicity is not a strong point in the Free Church. But literature about our missionary outreach is available – some of it attractive – and it is apparently not reaching its target, which is the heart of our people. Why are so many of us missing out, scarcely caring about witness overseas?

Maybe the personality (or theology) of some individual missionary (or Board member) does not come up to your standards.

Maybe some who have reappeared from the frontiers after years out of sight do seem a bit queer now. You don't want to be like them.

Maybe the gospel as we know it is good in our own culture but ..... In any case, Scotland is a mission-field today, and we won't think of other places (except when it's holiday time).

Maybe it is too difficult to think hard enough to distinguish the essentials of our faith from what is merely local. And it is too dangerous to move towards change of any kind.

Organisation is not the main thing, but perhaps it would help if the Foreign Missionary Association were revived. The W.F.M.A., youth groups, an organisation for men (why not?), support groups, including perhaps one for medical people – whatever a local situation demands – these could all be affiliated to the parent body. Coordination of activities would be important. This is another area calling for a full-time Foreign Missions Secretary.

Free Church Offices and College, The Mound, Edinburgh. (Drawn by Iain Mackay)

hunger – a parable

*"Well, **he'll** be hungry, even if I can't eat anything." Dr Vishwasi sighed deeply as she began to prepare vegetables for the evening meal. It was three months since she had come with her husband to this Scottish University city. Instead of beginning to feel at home, she disliked it more and more as the weeks passed.*

All had seemed so exciting six months before, when they were married at her home in Nagpur. He was to study for his post-graduate surgical degree in Britain and she would accompany him. Although it had not been possible to arrange for her to take a course of formal study, there was promise of a clinical attachment in her subject, Paediatrics. She had looked forward to setting up home for a few years in the West, with a degree of independence unthinkable in India.

*But if **this** was independence, she could do without it! Her husband was kind and considerate to her – no problem there. The generosity of her father and father-in-law, both wealthy businessmen, meant that their flat here was better furnished than some. Even so, she was miserable.*

*It was so **cold**! Everything was so cold! Rain in India was warm. Here, day after day, biting winds brought lashing icy showers. Gas fires dried their clothes – and gave her headaches.*

*Life was so **dark** too! Now, at 3 p.m., she needed the light on. There was not a hint of any colour but grey in the darkening scene outside: stormy sky above and stone buildings all around. Next week at home they would be celebrating the festival of Diwali – family and friends, flowers and bright lights, home-made sweets and savouries that might tempt even her jaded appetite.*

*Most of all, she felt **lonely**. Her husband left in the mornings while it was still dark and returned in the evenings, tired from a hard day's work at the hospital. After a meal he would study till after midnight. She admired his stamina and tried to encourage him, but she would have liked more of his time. Once a week she went to the hospital too, spending the morning on ward-rounds and in Paediatric Out-Patients. Clinical experience was good, although she found the accent of the English spoken difficult to understand.*

She understood enough of the conversation over mid-morning coffee to be thoroughly disgusted at the life-style of nurses here. (Perhaps some of the quieter ones did not have such shocking behaviour. But how could she know unless they became friendly and talked to her?) She used to think that Christians had good moral standards. Some standards in this "Christian" country! While at Medical School in India, Vishwasi and her future husband had declared themselves agnostics, although of course they remained Hindu in name. And for the sake of the family name, if for no other reason, no girl of her acquaintance would dream of living as loosely as the nurses here!

Vegetables ready, she turned from the sink and lit the gas stove. She tried to ignore the smell of cooking as she continued to prepare the meal. Today her youngest sister would have celebrated her tenth birthday. What fun they must have had! She pictured her mother and sisters, all on holiday from school or college because of Diwali. They would have spent most of the day preparing for the modest feast in the evening. How different from this lonely task!

When her father was a boy, his parents had fled from Hindu-Muslim riots in an area that became part of Pakistan. Although money and property had been lost, their business acumen was intact and, on settling in Nagpur, they had worked hard. Now the family – her father and his two brothers, with some of their sons – managed a successful enterprise there. Their home was a large modern house, with a good garden. With young cousins, nieces and nephews growing up, there was no shortage of vitality! She forgot her dreary surroundings as she relived happy childhood days at home.

The main dishes for the meal ready, she popped them into the oven and settled on the sofa to read. Her Paediatrics book demanded attention and stretched her mind. It was a less unhappy Vishwasi who served up dinner later that evening. This was one part of Western culture that she and her husband allowed themselves to enjoy – eating together. At home in Nagpur the men were served first and the women ate separately later. He teased Vishwasi gently: "Come on now. If you don't eat, our first child will be a weakling. And what were you telling me, after your ward-round two days ago, about the tiny baby whose mother confessed that she had not stopped smoking till he was well on the way? We mustn't let anyone think that you smoke!" To please him, she took a few morsels. It was a happy relaxed hour. Then he turned to his books.

Vishwasi was thoughtful as she washed up. She had been right. Hungry, he had enjoyed the meal thoroughly. Her hunger for friendship and understanding was satisfied too, at least for the present. Much of life was like a pregnancy. Starvation in its early stages could stunt any project. If those grandparents had skimped their input to the business in Nagpur they would not have been nearly so successful. She and her husband would not be here today, with the opportunity for post-graduate study in the West. He was not finding these first few months of his course easy. She must encourage him more. Smiling to herself, she determined to try and eat more sensibly also. Of course they wanted a strong healthy son. Or daughter.

Two points to consider:
Did we starve the embryo F.C.C.I.?
Are we friendly to strangers in Britain today?

17
And Now?

Although we may be too close to this century's work to evaluate it fully, we may profit even now from our Indian experience. Five matters seem to call for attention.

FIRST THINGS FIRST
In Adegaon one January, Mary Ann and I shared a room in the tiny house that was our base for winter camp. We had many laughs, not least over her insistence on doing "the high dusting" as often as sparrows reasserted their nesting rights above our beds!

My main memory is of her early rising for private devotions and of how she poured out her heart in prayer before and after her personal Bible reading. Another Hebridean lady, asked the secret of her gentleness, replied: "There is no secret. Only ..... I am always at Christ's feet, and he is always in my heart." Even if she did not like wearing a *sari* or eating hot curries, Mary Ann communicated the gospel well because she put first things first.

Devotion to the Lord – is this our priority?

CULTURE IS; AND IT MATTERS
In an article for the magazine "From the Frontiers" soon after her arrival in India in 1951, Mary Ann commented on how very ignorant she was about life and customs there. In Scotland, she had not been aware that such cultural differences existed.

Failing to recognise local culture, we erect barriers unwittingly to an understanding of the truth. "Does your wife wear a short frock?" some Hindu men asked Dr Raj Arole. They thought that no Christian could be a genuine Indian. Fortunately his wife, *sari*-clad, was close by, to show that being a Christian **is** compatible with being Indian! We talk of "a cultured person". But culture is not something extra – something additional to ordinary living. How we view the world: our different ways of doing things – that's what culture is. Just as each person, whether he knows it or not, is made in the image of God, so each of us belongs to a culture, whether or not we are aware of the fact.

We need to respect culture and be ready to learn a new one. For example, to eat with the left hand in an Indian village is seen as rude – only the right is considered clean. A person accustomed to wearing shoes when he goes to church may offend deeply if he does not remove them before entering a place of worship somewhere else. A beautiful Hindi version of Psalm 43 is set to a tune that seems strange to Scottish ears, while a tune dear to us in Scotland may sound weird and highly irreverent to an Indian listener. To adjust to local culture in such things is not only acceptable. It is kind and good, setting people free from the fear that by becoming Christian they would cease to be Indian.

No culture is to be accepted uncritically. Mention Scotland in any metropolis of the world – whisky, and so drunkenness, will come to mind. Materialism, the very fabric of Western culture today, has penetrated our church in Scotland far more than we are willing to admit. We must resist aspects of any culture that are wrong when judged by God's Word.

There is freedom in Christ, whatever the culture. No person was more free in mind and spirit than he. He submitted to restrictions for our sake. He is our example, as well as our Saviour and Lord.

OVERSEAS WITNESS DESERVES A FULL-TIME SECRETARY

Not only my own experience over the years in India, but also my research into the history of all three fields of our church's work abroad has convinced me of the need for a full-time secretary.

He would not be the decision-maker. He would advise the Board and would not have a vote there, so discounting fears of a Bishop. He would not necessarily be an ordained minister. Like today's part-time secretary, he would have missions on his heart and be able to get alongside workers, both national and expatriate. Not an expert in all aspects of the work, he would enlist the help of others.

His visits abroad, while not very frequent, would be less hurried than is possible at present, allowing more accurate assessment of a situation and more genuine encouragement as he would spend more time with people. In the home country, he would promote publicity and coordinate deputation work, sharing in meetings himself. He would get to know potential recruits and have a hand in their training. If he has a wife who shares his vision, so much the better. Going overseas occasionally with him, she might be even more welcome than he! Women missionaries would know that she at least recognised the awkwardness of their dual rôle – Amazon abroad, mouse at home.

Right through this century, as often as the question of a full-time secretary has been raised, the buck has stopped at finance. Have we got our priorities right?

RECRUITS NEED TRAINING

Probably I was not the only potential recruit to be discouraged by the lack of training on offer to Free Church missionaries. Would I be sent only as a Christian doctor who happened to be Free Church, or only as a Free Kirker who happened to be a doctor? It seemed to me that specific difficulties likely to be encountered by a missionary in India were not taken seriously. And once there, I felt keenly my ignorance of distinctive Reformed teaching. Listening to the guest preacher from America during a hill holiday in 1966, I was uneasy about what he said, but could not pinpoint anything wrong. Many months later, through careful listening to sermons in the Black Isle, I became aware of what the false emphasis might have been. I was able then to profit from relevant reading.

The Free Church already has her own College, preparing men for the ministry of the Word. If we are serious about reaching "the world out there", we should be using this College to prepare men and women for assisting in that work. Expertise in certain areas might still have to be gained elsewhere. But we missionaries need an application of Reformed theology to the whole spectrum of mission at home and abroad, including the diaconal part of mission. If we ignore this, we are virtually affirming that congregations should have only a one-man-ministry; and that our theology has nothing to do with physical matters.

TEST THE QUALITY

The very precious people who together make up the Free Church of Central India today are responsible to God for the quality of their Christian living. We thank him for them. It is time for us to test the quality of our own obedience.

When the door there was wide open, few men from Scotland were willing to enter. Opportunities have been lost. Are sons and grandsons being urged to **go** where doors are open today? Having entered, will they find people within earshot? The world is changing fast! Like Jesus Christ in Galilee, we must adapt our presentation of the everlasting gospel to make it clear to people **where they are.** Otherwise we might as well be miles away.

Those of us who did go are conscious of the poor quality of our faith and love. Now, back in Scotland, we appreciate good quality preaching in our mother-tongue. It is so precious that we go on thinking about the word long after the service is over. There was that address recently from Jeremiah chapter 13, about the linen belt ruined after being hidden away. God was talking about his very own people there! Refusing to listen, they became good for nothing. I wonder if God may be saying something like this today: "In the same way, I will ruin the pride of Scotland and the great pride of the Free Church of Scotland. They refuse to hear what I say. They persist in regarding their own comfort and material security as very, very important. All that I have given them with the purpose of advancing my honour in all the earth they are using selfishly." Could this charge be brought against us fairly as a church today? I think it could.

The one absolute standard in any test of obedience is our living, loving Lord. He wants us to demonstrate deliverance from the dominion of the darkness – every kind of darkness. By his grace let us speak humbly and eagerly, wisely and honestly, from the heart to the heart of our own generation, at home and abroad. And not only speak, but act.

"My soul thirsts for God, for the living God." (Psa 42.2)

"Jesus declared 'I who speak to you am he'." (John 4.26)

Appendix 1
Chronological Summary

1792: Baptist Missionary Society formed. William Carey sent to India.

1795: London Missionary Society formed.

1796: Scottish Missionary Society formed (initially called the Edinburgh Missionary Society). Their early missionaries to India included John Wilson, who arrived in Bombay in 1829.

1804: British and Foreign Bible Society formed. Sent workers to India in 1811.

1809: Edinburgh Bible Society formed. (In 1860 united with other societies to form the National Bible Society of Scotland.)

1829: Alexander Duff sent to India by the Church of Scotland.

1840: David Livingstone sent to Africa by the London Missionary Society.

1843: Disruption of the Church of Scotland. Free Church of Scotland formed.

1844: Stephen Hislop sent by Free Church of Scotland to Nagpur.

1869: Suez Canal constructed. Travel time to India reduced from three months to one.

1871: Seoni district transferred from the Free Church of Scotland to the Original Secession Synod.

1885: Indian National Congress (political party) formed.

1900: Majority of the Free Church of Scotland enter union with United Presbyterians. Minority continues as the Free Church of Scotland.

1903: First-ever public Christian worship in Chhapara.

1905: Elizabeth Macleod and Gilbert Dick, first missionaries of the continuing Free Church of Scotland, sent to Seoni.

1906: First issue of youth magazine "The Instructor" features Elizabeth Macleod.

1908: Alexander Dewar sent to South Africa, so recommencing Free Church of Scotland work there.

1910: World Missionary Conference held in Edinburgh.

1914-18: First World War.

1916: John A. Mackay sent by Free Church of Scotland to begin work in Peru. Concentrates on educational mission in Lima.

1924: Free Church of Scotland restarts work in India.

1926: Christian Medical Association of India formed.

1930: Present Chhapara Mission School built.

Population of Chhapara 4,000; of Lakhnadon 2,000.
1936: Lakhnadon Mission Hospital built.
1939-45: Second World War.
1944: Bible Society of India and Ceylon formed.
1947: Indian Independence Day – 15th August.
Church of South India formed.
1948: Mahatma Gandhi assassinated.
1951: Evangelical Fellowship of India formed. (Hindi branch in 1970.)
1953: Registration of all property in India required by Indian government.
1954: First visit of Foreign Missions' Committee delegate to India – Duncan Leitch.
1959: Prakash Kumar ordained in Lakhnadon to be minister of congregation of Lakhnadon and Chhapara.
1960: Population of Chhapara 7,000; of Lakhnadon 6,000.
1962: Dr Claire Thomson of C.M.A.I. reports her survey of Lakhnadon and Chhapara and advises expansion.
1966: Electricity supplied to Lakhnadon and Chhapara.
1967: Residential permits and "No objection to return" required by Commonwealth missionaries living in India.
1970: Church of North India formed.
Prakash Kumar visits Australia.
Emmanuel Hospital Association (E.H.A.) formed.
1973: W.F.M.A. prayer notes begun.
1974: Prakash Kumar visits Scotland.
Lakhnadon Hospital with Chhapara Clinic incorporated into E.H.A.
1975: Alexander John appointed headmaster of Chhapara Mission Primary School.
1976: McKenzies move to Jabalpur.
1979: Anti-conversion Bill in Madhya Pradesh.
1984: Prime Minister Indira Gandhi assassinated.
Visas required by all Commonwealth citizens in India.
1985: David John visits Scotland. Also Mr and Mrs Lalchuangliana of E.H.A.
1986: Presbytery of the Free Church of Central India set up.
1987: Free Church of Scotland property in India transferred to the Evangelical Trust Association of South India (to be held in trust).
1988: Population of Chhapara 12,000; of Lakhnadon 10,000.
Free Church Mission Education Society formed and registered.
Support groups in Free Church of Scotland take interest in Chhapara School and the Colegio San Andrés in Lima.
1989: No missionaries of the Free Church of Scotland now working in India.

Appendix 2
Biographical Notes – Orphans

Some details (accurate, as far as we know, in 1989) are now given of individual orphans. Not all came to be cared for soon after birth, hence the list is not in order of age. The year of birth is indicated by "b". If we know that the child was supported by a particular congregation this is shown by "s". Some who died early are not mentioned.

SURAJMUKHI (1922-?1943) helped care for younger children at Lakhnadon. Married, but died after the birth of their first child.

JAIWANTI (b 1932) trained as a teacher. Now widowed, she lives with her unmarried children near Dehra Dun, U.P.

PRAKASH KUMAR (b 1934: s St George's, Sydney) trained at the Oriental Missionary Society's Bible Seminary, Allahabad. He is the minister of the Chhapara Congregation. His wife Premlata trained as a Biblewoman.

PETER Macleod (b 1935) teaches in Chhapara Mission School. Married to Lila (see below). One of their sons, Emmanuel, is studying for the ministry of the Free Church of Central India.

ALEXANDER JOHN (b 1938: s St Columba's, Edinburgh) is Headmaster of Chhapara Mission School. His wife Sulochana teaches in a Government Girls' Middle School in Chhapara.

YAKUB (b 1942: s Buccleuch and Greyfriars, Edinburgh) drives a lorry at the Bhimgarh Dam site, ten miles east of Chhapara. Married to Rahil.

NAOMI (1939-1953: s Nairn) was drowned when a group of orphan children went to bathe and wash their clothes in the Wainganga River at Chhapara during the summer holidays.

PREMBATI (b 1940: s Duke Street – now Grant Street, Glasgow) is a teacher elsewhere. She and her first husband separated. She has remarried.

JOSHI LALL (b 1931) is the oldest in a family of four who came when their mother died tragically. Their mother was a Biblewoman at Lakhnadon, and their father a compounder. Joshi returned to stay with the father and we lost touch with him. Taramoni, Yunas and Chandra are the other three in that family.

TARAMONI LALL (b 1934) trained as a nurse at the Bible Churchmen's Missionary Society hospital at Kachhwa, U.P., and was greatly influenced by Dr Nevile Everard there. She is the Sister-in-charge of Chhapara Christian Health Centre and holds a lively Sunday School there. Her husband Panna Lall is evangelist-elder in the Chhapara congregation.

YUNAS LALL, or Innu, (b 1936) is Headmaster of the Government

Middle School at Dhuma. He is married to Lata (née Salve), who teaches in the Government Girls' High School at Lakhnadon.

CHANDRA (b 1939) is a teacher, married elsewhere.

SUSHILA (b 1933) trained as a teacher. Married in Jabalpur.

LILA (b 1936: s Kirkcaldy), Sushila's sister, is married to Peter. She teaches in Chhapara Mission School.

KRIPA (b 1943: s Brora) trained as a teacher. She and her husband (a grandson of *Bari Mama*) give hospitality in their home in the industrial city of Bhilai, M.P., to young people coming from Chhapara for training or employment.

SHANTA, or Chhotibai, (b 1946: s Lochcarron) took her nursing training at Kachhwa Hospital, U.P. Her husband, who had been an evangelist at Lakhnadon, became mentally unstable and violent. They have now separated. Shanta has the children, and nurses elsewhere.

SAMUEL MASIH (b 1946: s Hope Street – now St Vincent Street, Glasgow) is Alexander's second-in-command in teaching and administrative matters at Chhapara Mission School. He is an elder of Chhapara congregation. His wife Rajini is a staff-nurse at Chhapara Government Hospital. Their older son Sanjai teaches at the Mission School.

DANIEL MASIH (b 1946: s Hope Street – now St Vincent Street, Glasgow) is Samuel's twin brother. He too is a teacher at Chhapara Mission School. His wife Madhuri trained as a Biblewoman, and she also teaches at the Mission School.

(Angus) DAYAL MASIH (b 1946: s Kingussie) is registration clerk at Lakhnadon Christian Hospital and does some laboratory work also. His wife Salome is the nurse-in-charge of the Community Health team there.

DAVID TALIB MASIH (1948-1984: s Urray) wandered from home and remained unmarried. He died in Lakhnadon Christian Hospital.

YUNATAN, or Jonathan Faith, (1953-1957: s Dumbarton) died in early childhood, probably from malaria. His father had professed faith some years earlier but had not been baptised, nor stayed firm.

ASHOK ATUL DAS KUMAR (b 1954: s Dingwall) is a long-distance bus-driver with Madhya Pradesh State Transport. His wife Neelmani teaches at Chhapara Mission School.

KAMALA (b 1958: s Perth) trained as an auxiliary nurse-midwife. She is married to Apresh Dan, who proved unfaithful. Now separated, she nurses at Chhapara Christian Health Centre.

VIMALA (b 1958: s Aberdeen) is Kamala's twin sister. She trained as a Biblewoman and is married to Solomon Singh, a storeman at the Bhogpur Children's Home, a Reformed Presbyterian institution near Dehra Dun, U.P. Vimala is house-mother to children in hostel there.

ARUN DAS (b 1962: s St George's, Sydney) is a driver, married to

Neelmani, a staff-nurse. They both work at Lakhnadon Christian Hospital. SANTOSH DAS (b 1962: s Fortrose and Killearnan) is a driver and multi-purpose health worker, married to Rosemary, an auxiliary nurse-midwife. They also work at Lakhnadon Christian Hospital.

VINAI DAS (b 1963: s Lochcarron) wandered from home but is still in touch. He had been employed by a Muslim merchant in Itarsi, M.P. Early in 1990 he married a Hindu girl, his father having made the arrangement, near Chhapara.

VIJAI DAS (b 1963: s Dumbarton) graduated B.A., but unemployed. Hopes to work in a bank. Unmarried.

KIRAN (b 1963: s Kiltarlity) trained as a nurse. She is married to Silas Noel, a technician in ophthalmic work, employed in another Christian hospital in M.P.

SHARAN MASIH (b 1963: s Golspie) has graduated M.Sc., M.A., and is training in Hospital Administration. Unmarried.

MADHURI DAS (b 1968: s St Columba's, Edinburgh) is hoping to train as a teacher.

VINODH DAS (b 1969: s Kinloch) is employed as driver and multi-purpose worker at Chhapara Christian Health Centre. Unmarried.

Appendix 3
Biographical Notes – Missionaries

Name	Designation	Home Church	Location
BEATON Heather A	Nurse	Presbyterian Church of Eastern Australia Hunter/Barrington	Lakhnadon 1963-76 Chhapara 1982-85
BROWN Jane R (Janette) (Mrs A Gailey)	Nurse and Teacher	Free Church of Scotland Buccleuch and Greyfriars, Edinburgh	Lakhnadon 1947-50 Chhapara 1950-57
DICK Gilbert	Minister	Free Church of Scotland, Glasgow (from United Free, Dunblane)	Seoni 1905-06
DUNLOP Annie J (Nan)	Nurse	Evangelical Presbyterian Church of Ireland Botanic Avenue, now Stranmillis, Belfast	Chhapara 1944-75 (also Lakhnadon)
FERRIER Elizabeth (Mrs C Ferguson)	Nurse	Free Church of Scotland Free North, Inverness	Lakhnadon 1983-85
GILLIES Dolina R (Lena) (Mrs J A Brown)	Biblewoman	Free Church of Scotland Govan, Glasgow (from United Free, Earlish, Skye)	Chhapara 1930-44 (also Lakhnadon)
LUX Marie Christine	Nurse	Free Church of Scotland St Columba's, Edinburgh (from R.C. background in Belgium)	Lakhnadon 1982-83
MACDONALD Donald M	Doctor	Free Church of Scotland Buccleuch and Greyfriars, Edinburgh	Lakhnadon 1973-88
MACDONALD Mary Ann	Nurse Housemother	Free Church of Scotland Bernera, Lewis	Lakhnadon 1951-63, 67-71 (also Chhapara) Jabalpur 1979-80
MACKAY Annie M	Doctor	Free Church of Scotland Kingussie	Seoni 1921-25 Chhapara 1925-30 Lakhnadon 1930-66
MACKENZIE Catherine F (Darla)	Biblewoman	Free Church of Scotland Urray	Lakhnadon 1946
MACKENZIE Evan	Minister	Free Church of Scotland, Edinburgh (from Church of Scotland, North India)	Lakhnadon 1924-27

Name	Designation	Home Church	Location
McKENZIE Ian J	Minister	Free Church of Scotland Leith (from Presbyterian Church of Australia)	Lakhnadon 1964-68 Chhapara 1968-76 Jabalpur 1976-84
MACLEOD Elizabeth	Biblewoman	Free Church of Scotland Oban	Seoni 1905-25 Chhapara 1925-44, 47-48 (also Lakhnadon)
MACLEOD Flora J S (Mrs G A Neil)	Nurse	Free Church of Scotland St Columba's, Edinburgh	Chhapara 1962-68 Lakhnadon 1968-75
MACLEOD Kathleen	Nurse	Free Church of Scotland Stornoway	Lakhnadon 1973-77, 80-85
MACLEOD M Murray	Minister	Free Church of Scotland Dunoon	Lakhnadon 1933-49 (also Chhapara)
OLIVER W Mervyn	Lay Agent	Evangelical Presbyterian Church of Ireland Botanic Avenue, Belfast	Lakhnadon 1960-63
RAMSAY Helen M	Doctor	Presbyterian Church of Eastern Australia Manning River	Chhapara 1957-68, 76-85 Lakhnadon 1955-57, 68-70
STEWART Anna M (Mrs C Thomson)	Teacher	Free Church of Scotland St Columba's, Edinburgh	Lakhnadon and Chhapara 1938-41
STEWART Edith J (Mrs A J Dain)	Biblewoman	Free Church of Scotland St Columba's, Edinburgh	Chhapara and Lakhnadon 1935-38
STONE Barbara M (Mrs K Schmidt)	Nurse	Free Church of Scotland Helmsdale	Lakhnadon 1976-88
SUTHERLAND George	Minister	Free Church of Scotland St Columba's, Edinburgh (was Church of Scotland, Kintail)	Lakhnadon 1950-59
URQUHART Anne M	Doctor	Free Church of Scotland Killearnan	Lakhnadon 1962-74 Chhapara 1974-75 Satbarwa, Bihar 1975-76 Kachhwa, U.P. 1976-84
URQUHART William S	Doctor	Free Church of Scotland Fountainbridge, Edinburgh (later St Columba's)	Lakhnadon 1926-30

Appendix 4
Chart of Missionary Service

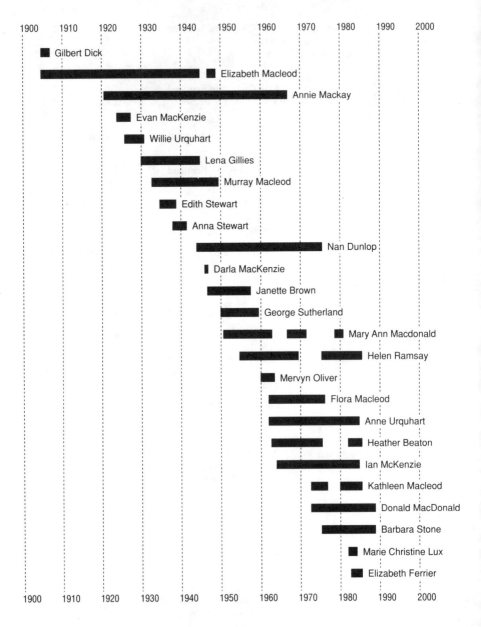

Appendix 5
Glossary and Abbreviations

1. Glossary

AYAH   Nursemaid.

BAI   Colloquial Hindi for a woman; a term of respect in M.P.

BAZAAR   Market.

BIBLEWOMAN A Christian woman trained to teach the gospel to other women and to children. Before 1950 she often taught in the *zenana* quarters of Muslim and Hindu homes. Instruction was in reading and writing in Urdu or Hindi, knitting, sewing and child care. Biblewomen were often *compounders* also.

BRAHMAN   A member of the group of people considered highest in the Hindu *caste* system.

CAMP   1. Evangelistic Camps: Until 1970, during the winter (November-February), evangelistic camps, with simple medical care available, were held annually in outlying villages. A few Indian Christians and one or two missionaries lived in tents or in a small rented house for about six weeks. Other villages were visited on foot, by bicycle, bullock-cart or jeep. Much preaching was done. Sales of Christian literature increased as literacy spread.

2. Children's Camps: Camps mainly for children of Christian families have been organised regularly from the 1970s during October or November, when there are school holidays because of Hindu and Muslim festivals. The leaders look after 10-20 girls for the first week and then about 10 boys for the second week, usually using tents or part of the *Toriya* buildings.

3. Eye Camps: A visiting ophthalmic surgeon brings his small team of helpers to the Christian Hospital at Lakhnadon. All are Indians. Over about four days, hundreds of patients are examined and dozens of cataract operations performed, with simple facilities. This work is subsidised by the Christoffel Blinden Mission, a German charitable organisation.

Government medical teams conduct similar camps, but more often for family planning operations.

CASTE A system of the Hindu religion which divides Hindu people into five groups: Brahman (priestly); Kshatriya (warrior); Vaisya (merchant); Sudra (menial); Outcastes, all people below the others. The last group are considered untouchable and were renamed *Harijah* ("people of God") by Mahatma Gandhi. Discrimination because of caste is forbidden by law, but is widely practised. Non-Hindus are reckoned to be outside the caste system.

CATECHIST A Christian man with some theological training, employed to evangelise. He might teach secular subjects in a primary school also. In the absence of an ordained minister, he would conduct church services. Catechists were often *compounders* also.

CHAKRA A small cart, seating 2 – 4 people, drawn by bullocks.

CHAPATI Unleavened bread, flat and round – about 7 inches in diameter. Made daily or twice daily, of wheaten flour, kneaded with water and cooked on a girdle.

COLLECTOR The chief Government official of a District. Also called the District Magistrate.

COMPOUNDER A man or woman trained informally to make up and give out simple medicines, to carry out certain procedures such as syringing ears and to help in the care of patients. The men especially tended to develop their expertise, often being regarded as doctors.

DISPENSER same as *compounder*.

EVANGELIST same as *catechist*.

EXPATRIATE A person living away from his/her own country.

HINDI The national language of India. (There are thirteen other main languages.) Hindi is spoken in North and Central India. When mixed with Urdu (as in the north), it becomes Hindustani.

HINDU adjective: having to do with Hinduism, the majority religion in India.
noun: a person adhering to the Hindu religion.

JI A Hindi suffix indicating respect.

JUNGLE A large expanse of non-agricultural land, covered with a varying density of trees.

MANTRA A set of words believed to convey supernatural power.

MELA A fair, usually held in connection with some Hindu tradition.

PATAIL	The headman of a village.
PUNDIT	A Brahman man learned in matters of the Hindu religion.
RAJ	A kingdom; popularly refers to the time of British rule in India.
SARI	The common dress of Indian women. It is a length of material (cotton, nylon or silk) measuring about five yards by one yard.
TEHSIL	The part of a District over which a particular law-court has jurisdiction.
TONGA	A horse- or bullock-drawn cart to seat 5 – 15 passengers.
VERANDAH	Usually at ground-floor level, the area along an outer wall which has been roofed over to give protection from sun and rain. If enclosed, it forms an extra room.
VERNACULAR	The local language of a particular group of people.
ZENANA	A place reserved for women (and children). Men may not enter.

2. Abbreviations

B.C.M.S.	Bible Churchmen's Missionary Society.
B.M.M.F.	Bible and Medical Missionary Fellowship.
C.B.M.	Christoffel Blinden Mission.
C.M.A.I.	Christian Medical Association of India.
E.F.I.	Evangelical Fellowship of India.
E.H.A.	Emmanuel Hospital Association.
F.C.C.I.	Free Church of Central India.
M.P.	The state of Madhya Pradesh, formerly Central Provinces (though their borders were not identical).
TEAR FUND	The Evangelical Alliance Relief fund.
U.P.	The state of Uttar Pradesh, in North India.
V.H.W.	Village Health Worker.
W.F.M.A.	Women's Foreign Missionary Association of the Free Church of Scotland.